ISBN 978-0-259-91100-5
PIBN 10836046

For support please visit www.forgottenbooks.com

1 MONTH OF
FREE
READING

at

www.ForgottenBooks.com

By purchasing this book you are eligible for one month membership to ForgottenBooks.com, giving you unlimited access to our entire collection of over 1,000,000 titles via our web site and mobile apps.

To claim your free month visit: www.forgottenbooks.com/free836046

English
Français
Deutsche
Italiano
Español
Português

www.forgottenbooks.com

Mythology Photography **Fiction**
Fishing Christianity **Art** Cooking
Essays Buddhism Freemasonry
Medicine **Biology** Music **Ancient
Egypt** Evolution Carpentry Physics
Dance Geology **Mathematics** Fitness
Shakespeare **Folklore** Yoga Marketing
Confidence Immortality Biographies
Poetry **Psychology** Witchcraft
Electronics Chemistry History **Law**
Accounting **Philosophy** Anthropology
Alchemy Drama Quantum Mechanics
Atheism Sexual Health **Ancient History**
Entrepreneurship Languages Sport
Paleontology Needlework Islam
Metaphysics Investment Archaeology
Parenting Statistics Criminology
Motivational

WILLIAM HUNTER,

ANATOMIST, PHYSICIAN, OBSTETRICIAN,

(1718-1783),

WITH NOTICES OF HIS FRIENDS

CULLEN, SMELLIE, FOTHERGILL,

AND BAILLIE.

BY

R. HINGSTON FOX,

M.D., BRUX. ; M.R.C.P., LOND.

LONDON :

H. K. LEWIS, 136, GOWER STREET, W.C.

1901.

K

HEADLEY BROTHERS,
PRINTERS,
LONDON AND ASHFORD, KENT.

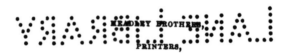

HEADLEY BROTHERS,

PRINTERS,

LONDON AND ASHFORD, KENT.

INTRODUCTORY NOTE.

———

of this work formed the Oration delivered
erian Society in London, on February 10th,
ublished in its Transactions; a portion also
columns of the *Lancet* for February 20th.

of the Society the Oration is now re-
considerable additions.

been a labour of love, continued at intervals
of years. The author's aim has been to give
ing of the life, works and place in Medical
whose fame has been too often eclipsed by
er brother, the great John Hunter.

part has been long in type, some want of
continuity has been found to be inevitable,
thor has sought to atone by providing a full
and Index.

London,

CONTENTS.

LIST OF ILLUSTRATIONS.

ERRATA.

Page 6.   Line 12 from bottom, omit " Soemmering and."

Page 8.   Last paragraph but one, read, " Hunter's first communication
       to the Royal Society was made as early as 1743," etc.
       See p. 53.

Page 12.   Line 2, for " 1765," read "about 1763." See p. 52.

Page 21.   Line 9 from bottom, for " 1812 " read "1784."

Page 22.   Line 3, after " whole " insert " periphery."

Page 23.   Footnote, omit " (C) "

Page 26.   Line 17, The sum for which Hunter purchased Fothergill's
       shells, etc., is variously stated. Lettsom states it as in the
       text. Simmons and Nichols give £1,200 ; Da Costa, £1,000.
       It was to be £500 less than the valuation.

Page 26.   Footnote, omit " (B)."

Page 27.   Line 4, for " twenty " read " thirty "

Page 30.   Line 19, omit " probably."

William Hunter.

WILLIAM HUNTER.

MR. PRESIDENT, AND FELLOWS OF THE HUNTERIAN
    SOCIETY,

I have thought that I could most fitly discharge the duty
which your kindness has laid upon me this evening, by
bringing before you the life of one worthy of your honour,
William Hunter, elder brother of John Hunter, after whom
this Society is named.

WILLIAM HUNTER, LECTURER ON ANATOMY.

In the London *Evening Post* for January 9th to 12th,
1746, there was to be read an advertisement in the following
terms :—"On Monday the 1st of February, at 5 in the
afternoon, will begin A Course of Anatomical Lectures. To
which will be added, the Operations of Surgery, with the
application of Bandages. By William Hunter, Surgeon.
Gentlemen may have an Opportunity of learning the Art of
Dissecting, during the whole Winter Season, in the same
Manner as in Paris."

This announcement followed the custom of that day, by
combining within the scope of one course of lectures,
Anatomy, the operations of Surgery, and the application of
bandages. The lectures were commonly given at the house

---

* The portrait of William Hunter is taken from an unpublished medallion in the
Hunterian Museum, Glasgow, by kind permission of Professor J. Young. That of Cullen is
from an engraving by Ridley, 1803. That of Fothergill is reduced from the fine plate by
Bartolozzi, prefixed to the third volume of his works, by Lettsom, 1784. Dr. Glaister kindly
permitted a similar reduction from the photogravure of Smellie (taken from an oil painting)
which adorns his Life.

of the lecturer, or in some convenient room elsewhere : but Nourse in 1737 set a novel precedent by holding his classes at St. Bartholomew's Hospital itself, "designing" he says in his advertisement, "to have no more lectures at my own house": his syllabus in 1748 included *totam rem anatomicam* in 23 lectures,—so limited was the knowledge of anatomy in those days. Later, in 1772, we find Dr. Saunders, and in 1776, Mr. Else, lecturing in the theatres of Guy's and St. Thomas's Hospitals respectively, but it was long before the custom of lecturing on the Hospital premises became usual. Thus Dr. James Maddocks, Physician to the London Hospital, lectured on the theory and practice of medicine in 1772, "in a large room in the Hotel, No. 5, Capel Court, opposite the Bank, in Bartholomew Lane." But the advertisement of lectures by Mr., afterwards Sir William, Blizard, and Mr. Thomas Blizard, in 1797, mentions their delivery in the Theatre of the London Hospital.

It was the retirement of Samuel Sharpe, Surgeon to Guy's Hospital, from his engagement of delivering an annual course of lectures before a Society of Naval Practitioners in Covent Garden, which made way for young William Hunter to take his place. Thus commenced his lecturing career in London, a career which lasted nearly forty years, and terminated only with his death.

William Hunter was at this time twenty-eight years of age, rather short of stature and slight in build, with delicate, almost feminine features, a refined, expressive face, and a certain notable brightness of the eyes. His address was pleasing, his words clear and precise, and he was fertile in illustration and humour.[1] He wore the wig, at that period in great use, even by boys at school who belonged to the well-to-do classes.

ORIGIN AND EARLY HISTORY.

William Hunter had been five years in London. He was the seventh child of a large family, John Hunter being the tenth and youngest, born in the old house, yet standing, of Long Calderwood in Lanarkshire. Of this family, four died in childhood at 1, 3, 14, and 17 years, and three at 25, 30, and 36 years of age—two of these from phthisis, and probably

---

1 "His dialect had all the polish of the Southern metropolis, with enough of the Northern recitative to preserve the close of his sentences from too abrupt a cadence," Adams, Memoirs of J. Hunter, p. 118.

others from tubercular affections,[1] one being James, a young anatomist of much promise : whilst three only lived beyond middle life—William, who died, gouty, at 65 ; John, died with aneurysm of the aorta, also at 65 ; and Dorothy, the mother of Matthew Baillie.

If as a family however, they enjoyed poor vitality, such members as lived were endowed with energy, industry, and talent far beyond the common lot of man. It is not without interest to follow the history of the stock a little farther. Of the ten sons and daughters, only two, John and Dorothy, left issue. Of John's children, two died young, two lived, but died without issue. Of the talented children of Dorothy Baillie, one, Matthew Baillie, never robust, died worn out at 62, leaving a son and daughter; the other two lived unmarried to 100 years or near it.

Extraordinary powers of mind are not uncommonly associated with a like strength of body, leading to prolonged old age, but the possession of genius is not favourable to the perpetuation of the species.[2]

The shadow of death, which had so often darkened the home at Long Calderwood, seems to have endeared the survivors to one another. Affectionate letters between the brothers and sister have been preserved : although in the youngest brother, John, the family bond was not so strong.

The father of the Hunters was a man of high character, and made many sacrifices to advance his children : his anxious disposition kept him, we are told, often awake at night, pondering his cares. He writes shortly before his death to his son William, who had had an offer of work in London, that nothing had proved a greater comfort to them all than the hopes of seeing him :—" I surely must soon expect to (leave this) side of time, considering my age and present Indisposition, being (for some) days past confined to my bed with sickness, and a severe fitt of (the) gravel, and would be glad to have you near me for the little while

---

1 Mr. W. Hunter-Baillie (who died 1894, aged 96 years), son of Dr. Matthew Baillie, used to say that those who died young died of consumption.

2 Descendants of Archibald, only paternal uncle of the Hunters, still exist; several have been in the medical profession. His grandson, the late Dr. William Hunter, of Largs, studied at the Great Windmill Street School, and became an army surgeon, being present at Waterloo. He married a sister of Sir David Wilkie, and died about 1874, aged over 80 years. Dr. William Hunter, J.P., of Rothesay, who died in 1893, was grand-nephew and heir to the latter, and has left children to inherit certain Hunterian heirlooms : another grand-nephew is Dr. Charles Buchanan Hunter, of Secunderabad, India.

(I may) be in this world, tho' at ye same time, I should be sorry to hinder you (from) making your way in the world the best way you can. I wish you (to) consider well what you do."[1]

William Hunter went, at the age of thirteen, to the University of Glasgow. His father intended him for the Church, but his enquiring mind did not readily accommodate itself to the unyielding tenets of the Presbytery. He became acquainted with William Cullen, then in medical practice in the town of Hamilton, a man eight years his senior in age; and spent three years residing as a pupil in his house, until he was 22 years old. They were, he tells us, the happiest of his life.

Hunter's choice of the profession of medicine was one result of this residence with Cullen. Another result was a lifelong friendship between the two Scotsmen. In an age when near relatives addressed each other as " Dear Sir," Cullen and Hunter are " My dear Willie," or " My dear old Friend," and the letters which have been preserved, for they seldom met in after life, form a valuable source of our knowledge of Hunter's true character.[2]

After a winter spent in Edinburgh attending the classes of Dr. Alexander Monro and others, William Hunter came, in the year 1741, to London. The journey was made by sea, and in the voyage from Leith they encountered a severe storm, and were in much peril of shipwreck.

He seems to have had but few introductions to the metropolis. The first was to Smellie, and at his house, or rather apothecary's shop in Pall Mall, he stayed for some time. William Smellie was like himself, an able, active, young Scotchman, ambitious of a wider scope for his abilities. Smellie and Hunter both became leaders in Obstetric Medicine in London. We shall have to compare their careers later on.

Another of Hunter's introductions was to Dr. James Douglas, the anatomist, and this proved of great value and importance to him. Douglas was an original worker of no mean repute; he is known familiarly to us all as the discoverer of Douglas's pouch, and he made likewise new and intimate dissections

---

1 Hunter-Baillie MSS., Roy. Coll. Surg., vol. I., p. 58.

2 See Thomson's Life of Cullen, vol. I., appendix.

of the peritoneum and its cavities. He was also an accoucheur,
and is referred to in the lines :—

> " There all the learn'd shall at the labour stand,
> And Douglas lend his soft obstetric hand."

Douglas was now approaching old age, and needing some
help in his anatomical work. He discerned the abilities of
young Hunter, and proposed to him to enter his household,
acting as tutor to his son, and assisting himself.

Hunter, who was seeking for the means of a livelihood,
accepted the offer, and lived with Dr. Douglas until he died
next year, and then continued to reside with the widow and
family. His relations with them were kind and intimate :
Douglas expired, wrote Hunter to his mother, with his
hand locked in his own.[1] In the meantime, Hunter attended
the classes of Nicholls, another famous anatomist, and was
surgeon's pupil at St. George's Hospital, then recently
founded. It is not unlikely that as Cullen had inclined him
to medicine, and Smellie had interested him in obstetrics,
so it was Douglas who fostered in his mind the liking for
anatomy.

It is as anatomist, physician, and obstetrician, that I desire
to bring Hunter before you this evening.

MEDICAL LEADERS IN 1746.

And here let us pause to consider who were the leaders
of medical science 150 years ago.

Sydenham, the English Hippocrates, had been dead for
over half a century ; Radcliffe for thirty years, and Dr.
Richard Mead, his successor, was now the leading medical
luminary in London. A coach and six carried Mead from
his country seat near Windsor to a town house, situated
where the National Hospital for Epilepsy now stands,
and in its galleries the Mæcenas of medicine had
gathered a library and museum of art which were famous
throughout Europe. Freind was dead, as was the accom-
plished Arbuthnot, but Sir Hans Sloane was yet living at a
great age, physician to the King, and the possessor of a large
collection of the curiosities of nature and art, destined to
form the nucleus of the British Museum. Huxham, who

---

[1] Hunter-Baillie MSS., II., 3. W. Hunter paid his addresses to Miss Douglas, but she died early.

had been a pupil of Boerhaave at Leyden, was in active work at Plymouth ; his tincture of bark yet holds its place in our pharmacopœia.

The most distinguished anatomist and surgeon was William Cheselden, now approaching old age. Percival Pott was in the early years of his work at St. Bartholomew's Hospital.

Looking abroad, eight years only had passed since the illustrious Boerhaave died at Leyden—*animum vix quisquam diviniorem, omnium amantem*—yet in the person of faithful pupils, such as Haller, then at Göttingen, De Haen, and Van Swieten, the great eclectic physician lived on, and the impetus he had given to the rational culture of the art of healing and its emancipation from the trammels of tradition was borne to many lands. The leading physicians in Edinburgh were disciples of Boerhaave, as were our own Mead and Huxham and many more. Friedrich Hoffmann and Stahl, in some sense rivals of Boerhaave, and each founders of a system or doctrine of medicine, were also dead.

The great anatomists of the two previous centuries, such as Vesalius, Fallopius, our own Glisson, Valsalva, Malpighi, and Bidloo, had left some successors. Ruysch, of Amsterdam, famous for his beautiful preparations, was not long dead ; Petit, of Paris, was yet living, though old, whilst Albinus, another pupil of Boerhaave, who occupied the chair of anatomy at Leyden for the long term of fifty years, was at the height of his reputation and activity.

In the department of pathology the science of morbid anatomy had been created by Soemmerring and Morgagni.[1] The latter was already old, but he lived many years yet, untiring in his dissections, and lecturing to his class at Padua to extreme old age. He published his great work, " De Sedibus et Causis Morborum," in 1761.

The science of botany was taking its first form and order under the genius of Linnæus, at this time at the height of his fame, Professor of Medicine at Upsal, and Superintendent of the Botanic Garden.

OUTLINE OF WILLIAM HUNTER'S LIFE.

We now return to William Hunter, entered upon his career as a lecturer on anatomy. He was so generous in

---

[1] *Der Begrunder der Neuen Pathologischen Anatomie.—*Haeser.

helping his friends from the fees he had received, that he found himself on the approach of the second session without the means of advertising the course.

In the meantime he practised surgery, having in 1747 become a member of the Corporation of Surgeons. In the next year he travelled on the Continent with young Douglas, going through Holland to Paris, and visiting some of the medical schools. In particular he went to Leyden, to Albinus, just alluded to, and saw some of the injected preparations for which that anatomist was famous, and was led to use this method of investigation in his own future work with signal success.

In 1748 his youngest brother John, ten years his junior, came up to London, fired, it would seem, by the same desire of a larger field for his energies. He wrote to offer his services to William as an assistant in his dissecting room. William replied with a kind invitation to visit London.

John Hunter became at once his brother's pupil and assistant, and was inducted by him into the anatomical studies in which he was to spend most of his life. He soon showed great skill in dissecting and injecting specimens, and assisted his brother in many of his researches in anatomy and physiology, making discoveries more or less in conjunction with him. These, as we shall see, were afterwards a fruitful source of dispute between them.

For several years after John came to London, his elder brother sought to direct and help him in his studies, placing him under Cheselden and under Pott. He even tried to give him what he had himself enjoyed, a University training, but John's stay at Oxford was very brief and to little purpose, and he referred very ungraciously in after life to the efforts that had been made on his behalf. Indeed, it must be acknowledged that the younger brother gave, for a good many years, little comfort or satisfaction to his friends. His manners were rough and coarse, and his associates low. Indications of this occur in the letters which have been preserved.

The dispositions and training of the two brothers were so different that it is hardly to be wondered at that they diverged as years went on. William, with his culture and polite instincts, had a trait of strictness and severity in his character, although he was kind at heart. Yet he refers often to his brother John in his lectures and in his medical

commentaries in appreciative terms ; and it was principally
through William's powerful interest that John was elected
to his most important appointment in the year 1768, that of
surgeon to St. George's Hospital.[1]

John once sent him a patient with the following laconic
note :—" Dear brother,—The bearer is very desirous of
having your opinion. I do not know his case. He has no
money, and you don't want any, so that you are well met.
Ever yours, John Hunter."

John left his brother's laboratory in or before 1761, going
abroad on account of his health as a Surgeon in the Army,
and was succeeded by Hewson, a very able young anatomist
with whom after some years William disagreed, and Cruikshank was engaged in his place in 1770. Hewson made
important researches into the lymphatic system, discovering
the existence of these vessels in birds and fishes, and demonstrating the human lymphatics with a fulness hitherto
unattained. He died at the age of 34 ; his works have been
published by the Sydenham Society. A curious letter is
extant from Benjamin Franklin, who, during his stay in
England, lodged at one time with William Hunter and
Hewson, and "as a common friend had been obliged to
listen to their mutual complaints." He writes to William
Hunter in 1772 to give evidence as to the terms of agreement between them.[2]

In 1750 William Hunter received his degree of Doctor of
Medicine from Glasgow University, gave up surgical practice,
and left the hospitable roof of Mrs. Douglas to take a house
in Jermyn Street, where he practised as a physician.

By this time he had made various communications to the
Royal Society ; the first was as early as 1743, when he was
aged but 25, on " The Structure and Diseases of Articulating
Cartilages."

At that time, and indeed throughout the 18th century,
papers on medical subjects were laid before the Royal
Society in large numbers. He was elected a Fellow in 1767,
in the same year as his brother.[3] It may be added here that
in 1768, on the foundation of the Royal Academy by Joshua

---

1 Adams (*Op. cit.*, p. 115) states that John Hunter's appointments to the army, and as
Surgeon to the King, were in like manner owed to William's influence.

2 Hunter-Baillie MSS., I., 126.

3 Tom Taylor, in his "Leicester Square," makes John to have received this honour ten
years earlier than William. It was really at an age ten years earlier.

Reynolds, Gainsborough, and others, Dr. Hunter was appointed its first Professor of Anatomy.[1] A painting in the Royal College of Physicians, of which he became a Licentiate in 1756, represents Hunter lecturing to the members of the Academy.[2]

In his practice Hunter had come to turn his attention especially to midwifery, and he had been appointed man-midwife to the Middlesex Hospital in 1748, and Surgeon Accoucheur to the British Lying-In Hospital next year. In this branch of medicine his reputation constantly grew, until in the year 1762, when he was forty-four years of age, he was called in to see the young Queen of George the Third. The story is told, but I have found no written authority for it, that the King asked him when he came out of the chamber, what ailed her majesty, and that he replied, "The Queen is *with bairn*." In any case his attendance gave much satisfaction, he was two years later named as Physician Extraordinary to the Queen, and from this date his practice amongst the upper classes rapidly increased. Hunter's polished manners and refinement, coupled with much shrewdness, and a careful attention to his patients, made him a *persona grata* with persons of rank, whether by title or talent. The letters existing prove that he was on terms of easy acquaintanceship with many of the nobility, such as the Earls of Chatham and Rockingham, Lords North, Bute, and Newborough. Horace Walpole writes to him in 1773 to promise him Lord Orford's "Orignal"—an American Moose deer.[3]

The historian Gibbon attended some of his lectures, and David Hume, little as Hunter must have sympathised with his philosophical views, was an intimate friend. A letter has been preserved, written in 1775 by the Bishop of Down and Connor, begging Dr. Hunter to use his influence with Mr. Hume, to prevent his coming to Ireland, where, says the Bishop, his character as a philosopher was an object of

---

1 The Diploma dated December, 1768, bearing George III.'s signature and the seal of the Academy, is displayed on the wall of the Hunterian Museum, Glasgow.

2 Hunter is demonstrating the muscles of the thorax on a living subject to an audience of about 25 persons. The artist is Zoffany.

3 Hunter-Baillie MSS., I. 128. I have to thank my friend Mr. T. A. Cotton, F.L.S., for identifying this animal: it is probably the specimen preserved in the Museum at Glasgow.

universal disgust.[1]   Eleven years later Cullen writes to
Hunter to give an account of Hume's last days, and gives a
striking picture of the calmness of the philosopher on the
approach of death.[2]

Hunter's character is placed in a favourable and interesting
light by some letters which passed between him and the Earl
of Suffolk, whose lady he had attended at her death in child-
bed in 1767.   Lord Suffolk had addressed to Dr. Hunter a letter
full of the most affectionate gratitude for his attention and
help: "My busyness is to beg of you, if *Reward* is an irksome
word, to let me substitute *Regard* in its room."   Dr. Hunter,
after warmly thanking Lord Suffolk for his letter, continues:
" I am now by your Lordship's kind sympathy, as happy as
I can be, after taking such a share in so great a calamity.   I
feel an inclination to say a thousand things which I must
suppress.   I wish to talk upon a subject which you must
forget.   We will take it up in Heaven.   At this moment I
fancy that I have a Friend there who listens to my thoughts,
and bids me say to you in a little time we shall all be happy
again ; who bids me tell you, to take care, for her sake, of
yourself and of your child.

"Allow me to love your child all the days of my life : she
will be exactly what you describe and what you wish.
Allow me sometimes to see her, that I may indulge a
pleasing melancholy and fancy that I am doing something
very agreeable to Heaven.   It may be preparatory to some
exalted enjoyment there.   Allow me likewise to offer your
Lordship the best advice I can.   As soon as possible, do a
force to nature and go into the bussy world again.   Nothing
but that, I think, can restore your peace of mind and make
you what I am sure you wish to be, a Blessing to Mankind.
May you yourself be blest, both for your own sake, and
for loving so tenderly one so worthy of all your affection."[3]

Nor was Hunter's acquaintance confined to his own
country.   He maintained correspondence with friends abroad,
sometimes in the Latin language, in which he was well

---

1 Ib. 89, 92.   2 Ib. 139, cf. 141, 142.

3 Ib. pp. 102-4. Henry, 12th Earl of Suffolk, K.G., was Secretary of State for the
Northern Department. He was devotedly attached to his lady, and after her death, cared
only to live for the child. She died at the age of eight years, and then Lord Suffolk married
again, though he could never shew again the deep devotion he had given. He died aged
only 39. The story of his loves and sorrows has come down through a favourite niece, who
lived to nearly 100 years, and told it to the present Countess of Suffolk, to whose courtesy I
am indebted for this information.

versed. At this time too, he was collecting for his Museum. The brothers Hunter were rivals in this also, that each formed a large Museum for teaching purposes. Anatomical preparations were the first object, but John, as is well known, added other departments of natural history, until he had drawn together the magnificent collection, which, enriched by later workers, adorns the Royal College of Surgeons in this city.

William Hunter took a yet wider range. Anatomy, healthy and morbid, was his first care. "The completeness," writes Professor John Young, M.D., the present Curator, " with which every organ is represented, in its normal and morbid conditions, indicates the systematic purpose with which he started ; and the exquisite beauty of the injections, vermilion and mercury, attest his great manipulative skill." Then Biology, in its whole scope as then known, was represented : stuffed animals, such as the elephant : and Hunter bought entire collections of shells, insects and minerals, as they came into the market. He included the spoils of Captain Cook's voyages, the weapons and implements of savage nations ; antiquities of all ages and climes ; books, not alone medical and scientific, but a fine series of the classics, and of early printed books and manuscripts, some of them illuminated.[1] His taste in art led him to obtain engravings, and a choice collection of specimens of the work of the best painters of all schools. Lastly his cabinet of coins, the object of unceasing care and lavish expenditure, contains 35,000 pieces, and is one of the finest known. The entire Hunterian Museum was taken to Glasgow in 1807 in accordance with Hunter's will : it has during recent years been well displayed in new quarters in the large University buildings in that city : but it is to be feared that its treasures are less known and used than they deserve to be. A proposal was mooted, a few years since, to sell the coins ; Mr. William Hunter-Baillie, then living at a very advanced age, viewed this proposal with indignation, and wrote that, as Hunter's heir, he should claim the money. The project was abandoned.[2]

He sought, but sought in vain, to construct on the basis of this Museum and his lecture classes a National School of

---

1 See for an account of the bibliographic treasures " An Address on the Hunterian Library, by John Young, M.D , Glasgow, 1897."

2 See APPENDIX (A), The Hunterian Museum, Glasgow.

Anatomy. He was ready to erect the building and to endow it with the sum of £7000. But his application in 1765 to the Government of the day to grant a site was unheeded, and the golden opportunity which might have done much for British Medicine was suffered to pass by. It was a bitter disappointment to Hunter, and although Lord Shelburne sought as an individual to undo the ill act of the Cabinet, and offered to head a subscription list with a promise of a thousand guineas, Hunter's pride would not stoop to accept it. He turned to rely upon his own unaided efforts. A plot of ground was purchased in Great Windmill Street, near the present Piccadilly Circus, and here in 1770 he built a spacious house, containing a large room for his museum, a lecture theatre, and dissecting rooms, besides rooms for his own residence. Here he lived and taught for the remaining thirteen years of his life. The house was afterwards occupied by his nephew Dr. Matthew Baillie, and it was here that his sister, Joanna Baillie, began to write her dramas : it still stands, a plain red brick structure, somewhat altered, the portico gone, and the building now incorporated in the Lyric Theatre.[1]

Hunter was a keen and jealous controversialist, laid exaggerated stress upon his own discoveries, and was too sensitive of his fame as an original worker. He was conscious of this weakness, an inordinate love of controversy : and condoned it on the plea that the passive submission of dead bodies rendered anatomists less able to bear contradiction.[2]

Vehement and bitter was his dispute with the Monroes, father and son. In the discovery of the tubuli testis, however, both he and they had been anticipated by Haller, who had announced his discovery before 1750.

Old Baron Albrecht von Haller, who had been Professor of Medicine and Anatomy at Göttingen, but was now at

---

1 The house of John Hunter on the East side of Leicester Square, containing his lecture theatre, dissecting rooms, etc., is at this very time about to be absorbed by the Alhambra Music-hall which adjoins it. An original drawing by Rowlandson, now in the Conservator's room at the Roy. Coll. of Surgeons, depicts "the Dissecting Room" of Dr. W. Hunter at Great Windmill Street. The large room is crowded : several bodies are exposed. Hunter's figure is raised above the rest : Hewson dissects an eye, Howison the intestines, whilst Cruikshank above him looks on, and Smollett's big form is seen, eyeglass in hand. Pitcairn, Baillie, Home, Sheldon, Camper and others have been supposed to be represented, but Baillie was not in London until six years after Hewson's death. Mr. J. B. Bailey, who has reproduced the picture in his "Diary of a Resurrectionist," identifies a figure upon W. Hunter's right with his brother John.

2 *Med. Commentaries, 1764, Introd. to Supp.*

Berne, one of the most estimable and illustrious figures in the annals of medicine, writes to William Hunter in 1764, sending a copy of his physiology, and refers to Hunter's dispute with the Monroes, in a spirit wholly above the littleness of controversies for priority : " He thinks himself happy in having such an able man of his same opinion." He goes on to speak of Hunter's unpublished work on the uterus ; he "longs after your performance of the fœtus whereof he would make a great usage."[1]

It is right to mark the failings even of the great, and this jealousy for the fame of a discoverer is one. Far better was the reply of Watt, when a friend regretted that another should have carried off the honour of discovering the composition of water : "It matters not whether Cavendish discovered this or I : it *is* discovered."

The dispute between the brothers Hunter, often alluded to, occurred in 1780, three years before William's death, and when his health was failing from gout. John had read before the Royal Society a paper on the placenta, in which he stated as his own discovery the determination of the separate maternal and fœtal circulations in the placenta. The work had been done twenty-five years before in William's dissecting room, and had been repeatedly and habitually put forward by the latter during many years past as his own discovery. For what reason John now revived this matter of ancient history and laid claim to the credit himself is not known. William promptly and emphatically protested in a letter to the Society ; and John replied in a cavalier tone, proposing that they should share the honour with all who were present when the dissections were made. The truth probably lay in some sense on both sides. The two brothers working in William's dissecting room, John, under William's directions, made discoveries. William may easily have regarded these as belonging to himself, and his obligations covered by a general acknowledgment of John's able assistance,[2] whilst the latter was disposed to claim them for himself.

---

1 Hunter-Baillie MSS. I. 114. Also Memorial of his death, ib., p. 158, "*pie et placide . . . obdormivit in Domino.*"

2 Such acknowledgment was often generous : he would say, "I am simply the demonstrator of this discovery : it was my brother's." Adams, p. 124.

The sharp controversy between these brothers, both so eminent, must have painfully impressed their friends, although the blunt, rough manner of the one and the sensitive pride of the other would go far to account for its occurrence. The Society decided not to print the paper, as it was in dispute. A sad estrangement resulted between William and John, and they scarcely met again.

After Haller died, Hunter was chosen in 1782 to occupy his place as one of the eight foreign Associates of the French Academy, one of the highest honours that a man of science can win. Haller's seat had been occupied before him by Morgagni, and before Morgagni by Ruysch. On this occasion the Chymists, one of the eight classes into which the Academy was divided, wished to have Bergman, the Swedish chemist, elected, but the class of Anatomists insisted that it was their right to appoint a foreign Associate, and Hunter was chosen.[1]

A letter announcing Hunter's election as a Member of the Academie de Medicine in 1778, in succession to Linnæus, bears the signature of Vicq d'Azyr.[2]

We do not find that either Dr. Hunter or his brother took much part in the political events of their time. A letter to a friend written in 1778, five years before his death, concludes: " I told you that I have taken my leave of Politics; and am sorry to say that as far as I am a judge this country deserves humiliation, or rather a scourge. God bless you. William Hunter."[3]

The times indeed looked dark and threatening. Great Britain was at war with the United States and with France ; Spain was just declaring war against us. The long contest in Hindustan was in its early and more doubtful stages. At home there was trouble and discontent. And who that could have foreseen the prolonged struggles that were to come during nearly forty years, would not have lost heart for the future of our country ? Yet through all, the staying power of the Anglo-Saxon race proved equal to the strain. William Pitt became Prime Minister in the year that Hunter died.

---

1 MSS. Miss Hunter-Baillie.

2 Hunter-Baillie MSS., I. 160, 159.   3 MSS. Miss Hunter-Baillie.

Ten years before his death, despite his frugal manner of living, Dr. Hunter began to suffer from "wandering gout," affecting, we are told, sometimes the limbs and sometimes the stomach. His bodily powers, strained by incessant exertion which he would not relax, gradually waned, but the spirit was active and undaunted to the end. On the 20th March, 1783, he rose from his sick-bed, against the remonstrances of his friends, to deliver the introductory lecture of his course, an occasion when there was a large and more general audience. Towards the end of the lecture he fainted, and had to be carried from the theatre. He never rose again, but died quietly a few days later, on the 30th of March. John Hunter came to see him again and again in his illness, and gave him needed surgical attention (catheterism). The brothers were reconciled at last. Dividing lines belong to life ; as it has been finely said, " It is death alone which integrates."

He died in peace. Life had had its storms, but the end was calm. "If I had strength enough left to hold a pen," he said to Dr. Charles Combe his executor, "I would write how pleasant and easy a thing it is to die." William Hunter was only 65 years of age, the same age attained by his brother John ten years later ; both died in the fulness of their work, closing a life of strenuous labour. So died their nephew, Matthew Baillie ; so died many other masters in our art, from the days of Sydenham and of Radcliffe down to those of our own Wilson Fox and Andrew Clark. He was buried in the Rector's vault of St. James's, Piccadilly, where his monument stands between those of Sydenham and Richard Bright.

WILLIAM HUNTER AS ANATOMIST.

I propose to place William Hunter before you as an Anatomist, as a Physician, and as a Practitioner of Midwifery.

Firstly then, and especially, as an anatomist, and in this term must be included throughout the work of the physiologist also, then scarcely separated from the sister science. The high place which is to be assigned to William Hunter in the history of anatomy is based upon four claims :—

First : That he was a close student of nature.

Second : That he made discoveries in anatomy.

Third : That he founded a school of anatomy in this city.

Fourth : That he trained his brother, John Hunter.

I will say a few words upon each of these heads.

(1) Very early in his career William Hunter formed the habit of mind which governed his whole after life, and made him an unprejudiced observer of nature. The words of John Hunter are often quoted, "don't think, but try"— yet this close study of nature by experiment was hardly a less feature of the work of the elder brother. At the age of 26, in a letter to his brother James, he speaks of "my dear idol nature, *simplex munditiis*," [1] and next year to his friend Cullen, he writes as follows :—"Well, how does the animal economy appear to you, now that you have examined it, as one may say, with precision ? . I have good reason to put the question to you, because in my little attempts that way, since I begin to think for myself, Nature, where I am best disposed to mark her, beams so strong upon me, that I am lost in wonder, and count it sacrilege to measure her meanest feature by my largest conception. Ay, ay, the time will come when our pert philosophers will blush to find, that they have talked with as little real knowledge, and as peremptorily of the animal powers, as the country miller who balances the powers of Europe." [2]

These are the crude remarks of a young man, yet how well they forecast his maturer thoughts let an extract from one of his lectures show. He is speaking of the middle of the seventeenth century :—"From that time the important doctrine of rejecting all hypotheses of general knowledge, till a sufficient number of facts shall have been ascertained by careful observation and judicious experiment, has been every day growing into more credit."

Observations such as these may seem to us to be commonplace, but they were not so in his day. The painted scaffolding of mere hypothesis, useful doubtless in its day, but which had too long done duty for truth—had too long hidden

---

1 Hunter-Baillie MSS. II. 11.   2 Thomson, I. 21.

the solid edifice which was within—had to be pulled down, piece by piece, in those reforming ages; and in this destructive as well as constructive work, William Hunter did yeoman service. His was an unflinching search for truth as it is found in nature. His life illustrates the precept of Bacon that "Nature is only subdued by submission,"[1] and that famous saying of Hippocrates, "Science and opinion are twain; the one makes for knowledge, the other for ignorance."—δυὸ γὰρ ἐπιστήμη τὲ, καὶ δόξα : ὧν τὸ μὲν ἐπίστασθαι ποιέει, τὸ δὲ ἀγνοεῖν.[2]

(2) William Hunter made for himself discoveries in anatomy.

The tubuli of the testis, the ducts of the lachrymal gland, the origin and use of the lacteal and lymphatic vessels, were subjects early investigated by William Hunter, with more or less assistance from John. William described in his lectures from time to time the discoveries that were made, and it was about these discoveries that, whilst John was at the war at Belle Isle and in Spain, William waged his controversial war with the two Monroes. Probably both they and he did good work in these departments of anatomy, though neither were actually first in time to establish new truths.

Congenital hernia was another topic which closely engaged William Hunter's attention. Haller had discovered and described it, but Hunter was the first to expound in detail its formation, in connection with the descent of the testis from the abdomen.

Again, he explained the anatomy of the different forms of aneurysm more perfectly than had been done before his time, and he minutely described the varicose aneurysm, a condition which had hitherto escaped the notice of surgeons.[3]

The discovery of the separate maternal and fœtal circulations in the placenta has already been referred to, as one in which perhaps both the Hunters had a share. Their description of the placental structure was questioned by later

---

1 *Natura non nisi parendo vincitur.*   2 *Nomos.*

3 *Medical Observations and Inquiries*, Vol. I., p. 323; II., 390; IV., 385.

investigators, but it has been justified by subsequent researches, and forms, I believe, at the present day the foundation of our knowledge of placental anatomy.

In close connection with this discovery must be mentioned his researches into the nature of the foetal coverings. Hunter first applied the name *decidua* to the membrane which lines the gravid uterus, and first described its disposition in that cavity : the decidua reflexa was unknown before his time.[1] The origin of the decidua was long a doubtful matter. John Hunter speaks of it as developed from coagulated lymph or blood, and gives a plate of it under that description. Even William Hunter is made to favour such a view in his posthumous work on the anatomy of the uterus, but the statement occurs, not in Hunter's own words, but in those added editorially by Baillie. Elsewhere in the MS. lectures which have been preserved, William Hunter states most clearly that the decidua is "a lamella of the uterus," "the internal lamellæ of the uterus itself."[2] It is clear, then, as Matthews Duncan shows, that John Hunter was wrong in this matter and William Hunter right.

Indeed, the closer William's own words in his lectures upon this whole subject are examined, the stronger does the impression grow that he had the principal part in the placental discovery.[3] Dr. Teacher tells me that his study of the preparations at Glasgow leads him to the same view, and that "the fulness and accuracy of William Hunter's knowledge of these structures was marvellous."[4]

But the crowning work of his life was the demonstration of the Anatomy of the Human Gravid Uterus. The book was published in 1774, when he was nearly 60 years of age, and contains thirty-four very large plates, mostly drawn by Rymsdyk. The typography is excellent, and is the work of Baskerville, the famous Birmingham printer. Hunter had been collecting materials for this great work for 23 years,

---

1 One of W. Hunter's plates of the decidua is still in use in Quain's Anatomy.

2 MS. Lectures, 1775, R.C.S., 42 c. 31, pp. 34-36.

3 Ib., p. 37.

4 W. Hunter displays a charming enthusiasm when he approaches the subject of the placenta. Holding up to his class an injected specimen, he says :—"Now let me set all modesty and all appearance even of it aside, and say here is the finest preparation in the world." MS. Lectures (cited), p. 27. He was extremely careful and jealous over his preparations: "There," he says, "is a fine preparation, and if you let it fall you may just as well knock me on the head, for I shall not be able to outlive it." Ib., p. 39. See anecdote by Dr. Parry, quoted in *Quarterly Review*, Jan., 1897, p. 113; but this was about 1778, when he was old and gouty.

having previously studied the subject in brutes. In 1751 he met with his first opportunity of examining a specimen of the gravid uterus in man ; it was carefully dissected, and the blood-vessels injected, and drawings were made and coloured by an able hand. In the course of some months, the first ten plates of his work were drawn, and were about to be published, when a second and a third specimen came in his way and furnished supplemental plates. He then formed the design of waiting, until, by embracing further opportunities, he might be able to construct a complete work, exhibiting all the principal changes that occur in the uterus during the nine months of gestation.

An admirable and unique series of preparations, from many of which the plates were taken, is preserved in the Hunterian Museum at Glasgow. There are about 400 specimens altogether, besides very fine plaster casts of many of the dissections. The collection has more than a historical value : it illustrates most graphically to-day the anatomy of the uterus and placenta, and proves how truly and fully William Hunter had discerned their structure and relations. And thus, sparing neither time, nor labour, nor expense, after twenty-three years he was able to bring before the scientific world his great work. The text is in Latin and English, in parallel columns. The plates are of much beauty and fineness of execution. They are nearly all of natural size, and are drawn with marvellous fidelity to nature, not allowing, as he tells us, the imagination to vary the actual appearances in order to render the object more useful as a demonstration—in other words they are in no sense diagrams, but as it were photographic in their reality. This will be easily understood by a comparison with Smellie's tables published some years previously.

This "immortal work," writes Matthews Duncan, "is one of the stable foundations of the science and art of midwifery, and cannot fail, in all future ages, to be as valuable and useful as it now is." It was reprinted by the Sydenham Society in 1851, and included in Caldani's Icones, 1813.

(3) A chief part of the influence of a great teacher is upon those who come after him. So had it been with Boerhaave : from Leyden, as from a centre of new light, the influence spread forth, so that in the early part of the eighteenth century a large proportion of the medical schools in Europe were led by those whom Boerhaave had trained. The pupils of the Hunter brothers were in a like manner

the leaders of British medicine and surgery at the beginning
of the present century. William Hunter's talents as a
lecturer were conspicuous. " He was probably," writes his
nephew Baillie, not perhaps an impartial judge, yet a writer
of much care and precision, " the best teacher of anatomy
that ever lived." [1]

"No one ever possessed more enthusiasm for the art,
more persevering industry, more acuteness of investigation,
more perspicuity of expression, or indeed a greater share of
natural eloquence. He was uncommonly ready in his
apprehensions, and singularly happy · in making others
understand what he knew himself. His arrangement of
any subject was clear and judicious ; he knew how far the
attention would reach, and when it was beginning to decline ;
and he had a most happy talent of introducing anecdotes
which might excite, amuse and instruct." [2]

The School of Anatomy which Hunter founded was
located in the house he had built, containing his museum,
lecture theatre, and dissecting rooms, and was hence called
the Great Windmill Street School. It was carried on after
his death, at first by Cruikshank and Matthew Baillie, and
after them by others, until about 1830. In the list of teachers
at this School we find the names of Sir Benjamin Brodie,
Sir Charles Bell, Herbert Mayo, Caesar Hawkins, Benjamin
Guy Babington. University College was opened in 1828,
and King's College in 1831 ; Bell migrated to the first, and
Mayo to the second, and the old School was soon after
closed. Its work was done, and Hunter would have rejoiced
to see the day of more ample and noble colleges, where
science has been taught in a far wider scope. But of these
colleges the old private schools, and this of Hunter's in
particular, were the forerunners and parents, and they are
worthy of parental honour. [3]

---

1 Baillie, *Autobiography*.

2 Baillie, *Lectures*, p. 74. The curious story of Mrs. Van Butchell, whose body was
embalmed by Hunter, long preserved by her husband, and is now to be seen in the
Hunterian Museum, Royal College of Surgeons, will be found in Pettigrew's *Med. Portrait
Gallery*, art. W. Hunter, p. 10. See also Sir George Baker's humorous epitaph :—
    " In reliquias Mariæ Vanbutchel, novo miraculo conservatas," etc.
            " Ab indecorâ putredine vindicavit
            Vir egregius, Gulielmus Hunterus
            Artificii prius intentati
            Inventor idem, et perfector," etc.
Quoted in Munk's *Roll of the Royal College of Physicians*, 2nd ed., II., p. 216.

3 On the Great Windmill Street School, see a letter by Sir B. C. Brodie, in Thomson, II.,
p. 740; and Mr. D'arcy Power's excellent article in *Brit. Med. Journal*, 1895, II., p. 1388.
See also Sir Charles Bell's *Letters* (p. 196, etc.); when he came to London in 1804 the
medical leaders were old Hunterian pupils (p. 20).

(4) The fourth claim of William Hunter to the position of a great anatomist rests upon the influence and training he bestowed upon his more famous brother, John Hunter.

It was said of Sir Humphry Davy that the greatest of all his discoveries was the discovery of Faraday, and so the greatest of William Hunter's was perhaps the discovery of his gifted brother. I would not indeed say, as Professor Gross does, that "if it had not been for William we never could have had John,"—nor quote, with Brodie, the claim of Ulysses to the glory of Achilles, *ergo opera illius mea sunt*: because one who reads John Hunter's works must own the marks of an original mind, which would have made its way, and taken its own course, had circumstances been what they might. Yet William's invitation of his brother to London, and his example and teaching during the years when John was his pupil and assistant, must have had a large part in directing John into the line of study in which he achieved such distinction. His was indeed, as Baillie writes, " a bold inventive mind," untrammelled by conventions or traditions, but seeking after truth alone. They were a great pair—*par nobile fratrum*; much of their work was common. We do well to honour them as " the Hunters."

WILLIAM HUNTER AS PHYSICIAN.

In speaking of William Hunter as a physician, I use the latter word in no restricted sense. Perhaps the departments of medicine were not then so strongly marked out from one another : at any rate Hunter took no narrow view of his profession. He began his medical life as an anatomist, practising surgery the while, then he took a physician's degree, and finally devoted himself chiefly to the practice of midwifery. Nothing, indeed, that came within the scope of medicine in its widest sense was foreign to his mind. He made many contributions to the six volumes of " Medical Observations and Inquiries," published between 1757 and 1812, by that " Society of Physicians " which was the precursor of the Medical Society of London, and is often confounded with it. Hunter succeeded his friend Fothergill as President of this Society. Several of the papers relate to aneurysm, and to his discovery of varicose aneurysm, others to the advisability of operating in empyema when there is no more than a reasonable probability of finding pus, to necrosis of the tibia and the nature of callus, and to rupture of the capsular ligament in dislocations at the

shoulder.   There is one very careful and elaborate record of
a case of traumatic emphysema, in which the cellular tissue
of the whole of the body was inflated with air.   The patient
was *in extremis*, but Hunter, by suitable incisions, pressing
the air out, and stopping the injured thorax, succeeded in
effecting a cure.   He goes on to expound the nature and
functions of the cellular tissue, and the use of punctures in
anasarca : these should be very small, rather than large, as
he had learned by trial of both these methods, one on each
leg of the same patient.   He had dissected black cattle, dead
of an epidemic disorder attended with emphysema.   Some
other papers deal with the structure of the symphysis pubis,
and the insensibility of tendon.

There are two remarkable papers on strictly medical
topics, both written late in life, and communicated to the
Society shortly after his death.   One records three cases of
congenital heart disease.   The first was of an infant, cyanosed
to blackness, which lived 13 days.   The pulmonary artery
was impervious at its origin, the ductus arteriosus bringing
blood to it from the aorta, and the foramen ovale was open :
the right ventricle contained scarcely any cavity at all.   In
the second case, an extremely thin boy, whose legs reminded
him of a greyhound or a water fowl, lived to 13 years,
subject to syncopal attacks; the pulmonary artery was
found to be stenosed, barely admitting a small probe, and
the ventricular septum was partly deficient.   This latter
condition obtained also in his third case, a still-born infant.

In commenting upon these cases, he enters on the
philosophy of malformations and makes the following
remarks : " The last conjecture which we shall venture to
make is upon the scheme which the Author of our nature
has laid down for perpetuating animals.   Particular evils
are allowed to exist.   Many animals, from the imperfection
of their fabric, are necessarily to perish before the common
natural period.   This is compensated for by a great superfluity
in the number, and so it is also in the Vegetable Kingdom.
As in vegetables too, the parent generally produces a species
very like itself : but sometimes a different constitution,
whether better or worse.   Whatever may happen in a
particular instance, or with regard to an individual, the
most perfect and sound animal upon the whole, will have
the best chance of living to procreate others of his kind : in
other words, the best breed will prevail : and the monstrous
constitution, and that which is defective, or of such a fabric

William Cullen.

as necessarily to breed disease, will be cut off. The most perfect constitution will be preserved : it will be most susceptible of love, and most likely to meet with a warm return of that passion: so that, in every way, the sound constitution will have the preference in procreation, and the defective, weak, or diseased line will be wearing out."[1]

In these remarkable sentences we see a foreshadowing more than 100 years ago of the doctrine of Evolution. The essential influence of Natural Variation and the Survival of the Fittest, two of the most prominent features of the Darwinian theory, are clearly stated by William Hunter. /

The other paper is not less noteworthy.

It treats of "the successful cure of a severe disorder of the Stomach by Milk taken in small quantities at once."[2] A boy of seven or eight years was reduced to a desperate condition on account of vomiting his food. He was wasted to a mere skeleton, and had been in the hands of many doctors. Hunter hit on the happy expedient of giving milk alone, and reducing the dose to such a modicum as he could retain. This case is often quoted, and is given at large by Sir Thomas Watson in his lectures.[3]

I must allude to one more of Hunter's papers, that on the "Uncertainty of the Signs of Murder in the case of Bastard Children." This paper, which shows that legal medicine also engaged his thoughts closely at times, deals with the delicate and difficult question of the guilt of a mother for child-murder or concealment of birth, and of the proofs of her crime. Hunter's long experience and wide knowledge of mankind, his high sense of justice, and his deep sense of pity are alike displayed in this remarkable paper, which is well worthy of study at this day.[4]

WILLIAM CULLEN.

It may be appropriate here to say something of two eminent friends of William Hunter, William Cullen and John Fothergill. Cullen has already been alluded to as his early preceptor in medicine, and throughout life his constant and affectionate friend. He was eight years Hunter's senior, but he attained a much greater age, outliving Hunter by seven years. It is hardly necessary to describe the high

---

[1] *Med. Obs.*, VI., 307.   [2] Id. p. 310.   [3] *Lecture* lxviii.

[4] *Med. Obs.*, VI., 266. This paper was reprinted in the third edition of Dr. Samuel Farr's "*Elements of Medical Jurisprudence*," 1815. An exquisitely written MS. copy is in the Library of the Roy. Med. Chir. Society. See APPENDIX (C).

position attained by Cullen as a medical teacher. He lectured from 1746 to 1790, for the first ten years at Glasgow, and afterwards at Edinburgh. His fame as a lecturer was very great and well deserved. We are interested here in the comparison between Cullen and Hunter. Closely attached as they were, and consulting together often by letter, their aims in medicine differed somewhat widely. Cullen was of the philosophical school: he took medicine as it was then known, and threw it into systematic shape. He probably did not add, writes Sir William Hamilton, "a single new fact to medical science." By the medium of his lectures, delivered extempore, the principles of the medical art were promulgated in an ordered form and sequence which was evolved by his clear and able mind. Such a teacher must pass over inconsistencies and difficulties, must adopt hypotheses, and can scarcely avoid giving them the emphasis of proven facts, and cannot use that suspension of judgment in matters as yet undetermined which was the attitude of the Hunters. His system, his methodical synopsis of medical knowledge, was admirable for teaching purposes, but its rigid lines tended afterwards to cramp and hinder the very science which at first they promoted; and the greater the ability with which a system has been framed, and the higher its consequent authority amongst men, the longer does it exert its contracting influence over the progress of knowledge.

It was long before Cullen published anything, not indeed until pirated copies of his lectures were being issued by others. When in 1776 he found himself compelled to print, he sent his MSS. up to Hunter in London, begging for his revision and advice. Hunter returned them with a kindly letter.

"I have read them," he writes, "with care, and shall speak with freedom. I am sensible of no material objection to your doctrines. I have not yet made up my mind about many of the phenomena, particularly about inflammatory crusts, exsudation, pus, expectoration, etc., and, therefore, I cannot in some of these questions decide with you or against you."[1]

John Hunter had not yet laid down what has been termed by Latham the grammar of inflammation. A methodical teacher like Cullen *must* make up his mind on all these

---

1 Thomson, I. 559.

John Fothergill.

points, and it is not always to the furtherance of the truth. His systematic works continued to be used as text books for at least forty years after his death.[1]

JOHN FOTHERGILL.

Another friend of William Hunter's was Dr. John Fothergill. There was something of a parallel in the outward course of their lives. Each came up to London as a young man unknown, Hunter from Scotland, Fothergill from the Yorkshire dales; each set himself to a life of continuous work and research, each attained to fame and honour and large emoluments, and each died unmarried about the same age.

Fothergill was an assiduous and zealous clinical worker: he lived first in Gracechurch Street, and afterwards in Harpur Street, Bloomsbury. His opportunity came in the epidemic of "putrid sore throat" as it was called, which broke out in many parts of Europe in the years following 1747; it is generally considered to have been identical with the "diphtheria" of Bretonneau. Fothergill studied this disease minutely, and was very successful in its treatment. His practice as a physician at once rose, until he could hardly meet the demands made upon him. His treatise upon the disorder is one of our British medical classics.

He was a consistent member of the Society of Friends, a Quaker of the old school, subdued in spirit, cautious in expression, singular in speech, benevolent towards all men. He was Clerk of the Friends' Yearly Meeting one year, and he devoted time and thought, in conference with Dr. Franklin, to draft a scheme for overcoming the dispute with the American colonies without recourse to war.

In a day when good schools were uncommon, he took the chief part in founding a large school at Ackworth in Yorkshire, where his memory is still lovingly cherished; a school which has done excellent work, both within his own community and beyond its borders.

Fothergill had this especially in common with William Hunter, that both were ardent lovers of natural history. The vegetable kingdom was perhaps his chief field. His botanical garden at Upton was esteemed the best in Europe after that at Kew, and was stocked with the choicest plants from abroad. He had agents in every part of the known world collecting new and rare living specimens. A letter

---

1 Thomson's edition of his works is dated 1827.

has been preserved which is said to be in the handwriting of the young Queen of George the Third. It is dated from Richmond Lodge, Sept. 11th, 1769, and runs thus :—

"Mrs. Schwellenberg's Compliments to Doctr. Hunter and she heard yersterday that Doctr. Forthergyll had got several Tea Trees Come from the Indieas in the Last Ships and the Queen wishes that Doctr. Hunter Could make Interest with Doctr. Forthergyll to get Her only one of them for Her Majestys own Garden."[1]

Fothergill died a few years before Hunter, and seventy mourning coaches followed the body to its sequestered and beautiful resting place at Winchmore Hill. His collection of paintings of flowers and other natural objects on vellum was purchased for the Empress of Russia for £2,300 ; and his shells, corallines, insects, reptiles, etc., were offered at his express desire to his friend William Hunter for the sum of £1,500, far below their cost, and they now form part of the Museum at Glasgow.[2]

MATTHEW BAILLIE.

In considering Hunter as a physician it is natural to think of his nephew, Dr. Matthew Baillie. He was the only son of Dorothy Hunter, who married the Rev. James Baillie, afterwards Professor of Divinity at Glasgow. His father dying whilst he was still a youth, young Baillie was adopted by William Hunter, who, however, treated him with a certain strictness which was no doubt judged expedient for his training. He gave him an excellent education, first at Glasgow, then at Oxford, and finally in London. Classical exercises formed an important feature ; he had to send to his uncle from time to time long passages of Latin prose of his own construction. The details of his study were supervised by William Hunter ; he was kept well in his place, and rather "pinsh'd for money." "First deserve, then expect" was his uncle's emphatic injunction.[3]

When he came to London, about three years only before his uncle's death, he became at once his pupil, availing himself at the same time of the best facilities for studying elsewhere. Baillie entered quickly into the Hunters' methods, his training had already made him accurate and methodical, and when Hunter died in 1783, the young man of twenty-two stepped at once into his place, and, in conjunction with

---

1 Hunter-Baillie MSS. Vol. 1., 118. 2 See Appendix (B) *Dr. John Fothergill.*
3 H.-B. MSS., II., 4, 21, etc.

Matthew Baillie.

Cruikshank, advertised the continuance of the anatomical lectures. It was a bold step, but well justified by the result.

William Hunter had left him his house, and the use of his fine museum for twenty years, after which it was to go to Glasgow. Of the £19,000 which constituted his uncle's fortune, £8,000 was bequeathed for the support of the museum, and other sums as annuities to relatives, so that a comparatively small residue came to Baillie, besides the old Hunter property at Long Calderwood, which he generously relinquished in favour of his uncle John.

Baillie's classes were soon well attended, and for sixteen years he worked assiduously as a medical teacher, dissecting, comparing, lecturing and writing. Morbid Anatomy was his chief occupation, and his steadfast aim was to make this the basis of his clinical work. In the meantime he had been elected, partly through John Hunter's influence, physician to St. George's Hospital. By the year 1800—he was then but 39 years old—his private practice had so greatly increased, that he retired, first from the lectureship and then from the hospital appointment, and devoted himself to his consulting practice alone. This was probably the largest known in London since the days of Mead. He enjoyed the leading position for about twenty years, and was the trusted attendant of King George the Third and his family, and their confidant in their secrets and troubles, which were many. A baronetcy was offered to him about 1812, but he preferred, it would seem, to remain with Harvey and Sydenham and Mead and the Hunters, undistinguished by the titles which have given to some lesser men a brief and borrowed lustre. Like his uncle, Matthew Baillie was a man of slender frame, never robust; his sisters lived to nearly 100 years, and his own life might have been longer had it been one of less pressure, but under the unceasing toil, sixteen hours daily, his mind was harassed and his energies exhausted, so that he died, literally worn out, in 1823, at 62 years of age. He was a man of singular integrity, and guileless simplicity of character, and so bore himself through all the duties of life, which were in his case fraught with wide influence on others, as to win the confidence and admiration of all men.[1]

I have yet to speak of one notable event in Dr. Baillie's life—his publication in 1793 of a treatise on Morbid Anatomy. I think that the importance of this event as

[1] See *Memoir* by his son, in *Hunter-Baillie* MSS. II., 80. His *Autobiography* was edited by Mr. J. B. Bailey and published in the *Practitioner*, July, 1896.

marking an era in the history of medicine is hardly yet
appreciated. It was, so far as appears, the first systematic
treatise on Morbid Anatomy that had been written in any
country. Morgagni in his famous work, *De Sedibus et
causis Morborum*, published in 1761, had given to the
world a series of records of cases and dissections which
forms a storehouse of facts. Soemmerring had done similar
work. But Baillie for the first time took the various organs
of the body *seriatim*, and set forth the diverse morbid conditions which were found to belong to each. The basis of
the work was his own observation, his own specimens and
preparations, and those which his uncle had made before
him. And the whole was written with such candour and
simplicity and clearness of diction, as to be a model for all
future writers in the same field. When he does not know
the cause of any lesion he does not hesitate to say so : here
are no hypotheses to mislead, no traditional maxims which
will one day have to be unlearned. Well might the Pathological Society at its origin in 1846 place the bust of this
first of British pathologists upon its seal. And well justified
are those words which grace his monument in Westminster
Abbey, " *Qui ad certiorem rationis normam, eas anatomiæ
partes, quæ morbos spectant, primus redegit.*"

Brodie, writing at least fifty years after its first issue,
states that Baillie's work "is still the most valuable text-
book on that subject that exists . . . It is perfect as far
as it goes." [1]

I do not know that it would be possible to illustrate in a
more striking manner the place and influence of the
Hunters in the development of Medical Science than by
contrasting two works, issued at but thirty years interval.
Let us take Gaubius's Pathology, the work of a man accounted
a leader—he succeeded his master Boerhaave at Leyden—
and he was even a reformer, so that he excuses himself in his
preface for the innovations he has made. It was published
in 1761, and is an able book, yet full of vague generalities
and ideas which have come down by tradition. And these
are his closing words, "Unless I am mistaken his authority
will remain to Hippocrates, credit to Galen, strength and
order to Nature."— *Ni fallor, Hippocrati auctoritas sua
constiterit, Galeno fides, naturæ virtus et ratio.*

---

[1] Autobiography, p. 187.

William Smellie.

Compare with this Baillie's Morbid Anatomy, issued in 1793. To pass from Gaubius to Baillie is like going out of darkness into light. And this advance in Medical Science, fruitful presently in better medical art, was due, as I submit, mainly to the Hunters, whose anatomical and physiological work Baillie continued and carried into the domain of pathology and medicine.

WILLIAM HUNTER AS AN OBSTETRICIAN.

The art of midwifery was passing in the middle of the eighteenth century through a severe struggle. When Smellie settled in London in 1739 the bulk of the practice was in the hands of midwives. Mrs. Nihell, of the Haymarket, who afterwards published a treatise on the subject, had a large practice, and was a doughty and uncompromising champion of the exclusive right of her own sex to practise the art. Between her and Smellie, who lived hard by in Pall Mall, there was unceasing war. There were indeed men physicians devoted to this art, but when they were called in it was often only to advise the midwife, the patient not permitting herself to be touched. When William Hunter attended the young Queen of George III. he merely waited in an ante-room in case the midwife needed his assistance. The principal men-midwives when Smellie and Hunter began to work were Dr. Maubray and Sir R. Manningham. Of the former it need only be mentioned that he stated a decided preference for a seven months' over a nine months' gestation, on account of the influence of the moon and the mystical value of the number seven. Manningham was of a better order, and long enjoyed a high reputation in London, where he founded the first maternity institution. He detected the imposture of Mary Tofts, the "rabbit-breeder." Yet so far was the art in its infancy that in his compendium, published in the year that Smellie commenced practice, no mention is made of any sort of instruments. Instruments, however, were in use, but mainly of a destructive kind, and it was Smellie's earnest desire to find better methods, so that in difficult cases the child's life should not be sacrificed, that brought him to London.

WILLIAM SMELLIE.

It will be convenient to say a little more here of William Smellie, who has found in recent years so excellent a *vates sacer* in Dr. Glaister, to whose work I am indebted for much information.

He came from the same county as the Hunters and Cullen, having been born in Lanark some twenty years before William Hunter. Engaged at first in general practice in his native town, he took a keen interest in midwifery work, and came to London, as has already been said, to seek for improvements in his practice and methods. He went to Paris to Gregoire, then in much fame, but he was disappointed in him and in the other French teachers. Smellie settled in London in 1739, and practised and taught midwifery to large classes. His success was great; he had mechanical genius, and he studied the use of the forceps, then newly invented by the Chamberlens, until he had mastered the subject. He was the first writer to lay down rules for the safe application of the forceps, and as such is entitled to the gratitude and honour of all men. William Hunter, who was conservative in his midwifery practice, discouraged its employment, although he probably used it sometimes; he would say that he rather regretted the invention of the instrument, as he thought it had done more harm than good. Partly in consequence of Hunter's teaching, the use of the forceps, which had obtained a good deal of currency in Smellie's time, fell into disfavour towards the end of the eighteenth century, until Baudelocque and others restored it to its rightful place.

Smellie was uncultured, and unpleasing to those of polite manners, so that he never acquired large practice amongst the upper classes, skilful practitioner though he was. He tells us that in one labour, "I sweated so much that I was obliged to throw off my waistcoat and wig, and put on my nightgown, with a thin napkin over my head." I know not how far our leading obstetricians of to-day would regard this as a dignified costume. William Hunter, on the other hand, was urbane and conciliatory, and was singularly calculated for the practice of midwifery, Baillie tells us, "by the delicacy of his manners, and a very quick perception of the caprices of the world."[1]

Smellie retired from London to end his days quietly in Lanark, (where the battered remnants of his library,

---

1 *Lectures,* p. 75. Compare the "Eloge" upon W. Hunter in the Académie Royale des Sciences. "Il fut très-heureux pour les Dames Angloises, que M. Hunter unît à une habileté pour le moins égale, la douceur et les agrémens dont l'austère et savant Smellie avoit été privé," quoted in *Memoir of Smellie, New Syd. Soc.*

bequeathed for the benefit of the town, are still to be seen), revising his collections of cases, and publishing them to the world. For some years before this, he and Hunter, once intimate, had somewhat diverged, and Hunter tried in vain to arrange an interview between them before the former departed. Smellie avoided it, and wrote a curious letter from his Scottish retreat to Dr. Clephane, a mutual friend, to explain his reasons, quaintly dating his epistle from Tartarus, and addressing those still in the land of the living. He was evidently afraid of Dr. Hunter, whose quick wit and "glib tongue" would soon get the better of a silent man, without any conversational powers outside his professional work. He sent also a "letter of exculpation," a very singular and candid description of his own character.[1] Smellie was a great practitioner and an admirable man, and probably furthered the progress of his art more than any other single man in his century. He died childless in 1763.

William Hunter was for many years the acknowledged leader in obstetric practice in London. In dealing with his claims to distinction in this department, I am glad to be able to quote one who wrote with authority, the late Dr. Matthews Duncan. In his "Researches in Obstetrics" (1868), Dr. Duncan quotes Dr. Hunter many times; for example :—On the inclination of the axis of the uterus, the plasticity of the uterus adapting itself to the shape of the fœtus, the condition of the cervix during pregnancy, the cause of the fœtal head being commonly downward, the especial development of the cephalic end of the fœtus, the posture of the child during the last months of gestation, the early implantation of the placenta over the cervix, the separation of the fœtal from the maternal portion of the placenta in a four months' conception, and the operation of symphyseotomy.

Smellie acknowledges the help derived from Hunter's "reforming the wrong practice of delivering the placenta," i.e. leaving it more to natural efforts. And Hunter's lectures, preserved to us in the notes of students, bear witness to his thorough grasp of the practical issues of his art. He describes for instance, clearly and simply, the occurrence of fever, convulsions, white leg, hemiplegia, etc., in the puerperal

---

1 See the letters, discovered by Prof. J. Young, M.D., *Brit. Med. Journal*, 1896, II. p. 514. A short letter from Smellie to W. Hunter is in the *Hunter-Baillie* MSS., I. 110. Dr. Glaister informs me that one of Smellie's original class tickets has lately been discovered in the Boston Library, U.S.A.

state, and his treatment, if rather conservative and inactive, is at any rate free, alike from active hurtfulness, and from a pretence of specifics.[1]

Hunter described the retroversion of the gravid uterus apparently for the first time, and proposed the name by which the displacement is now known. His papers on this subject are very clear and interesting.[2]

WILLIAM HUNTER'S PERSONAL CHARACTER.

A few words remain to be said on William Hunter's personal character. His many-sided tastes have been referred to. It is wonderful, perhaps, that they did not hinder him from attaining high distinction in his own profession. But he had no wife nor child, and his museum was the recreation of his leisure hours. A man of untiring industry, an early riser, exact and orderly in his habits, thoughts and speech, he combined the learning of a scholar with the refined manners of a gentleman. He was kind, and he was just: and if he was so conscious of his own abilities, and so sensitive to praise or blame, that he sometimes appeared jealous, sometimes even bitterly combative in his attitude to others, such feelings did not long disturb his peace of mind. "I am I believe one of the happiest of all men," he writes to Cullen in 1768, "though my hurry is somewhat greater than I could wish."[3]

Of the vein of quaint humour which pleasantly varied the course of his lectures, I may give one illustration. It was in 1775, at the close of the session—he was approaching his sixtieth year: "I have now finished," he said, "twenty years of lectures. However, as I presume I am still approved of, I propose twenty years more to begin next October, and after this is over, I propose to settle in the world and take to me a wife."[4]

He was one who

> " preserved from chance control
> The fortress of his 'stablisht soul ;
> In all things sought to see the whole ;
> Brooked no disguise ;
> And set his heart upon the goal,
> Not on the prize."[5]

1 M.S. Lectures, R.C.S. 42. b. 34.   2 *Med. Obs.* IV. 400, V. 388.
3 Thomson, I., 554.   4 M.S. Lectures, 42, c. 31.
5 W. Watson on Matthew Arnold.

I have thus sought to set William Hunter before you as a great anatomist, and as a sound and successful practitioner of medicine and midwifery.

"Verax : capax, perspicax : sagax, efficax : tenax."[1]

A teacher of renown and wide influence, he contributed greatly, with his brother John Hunter, to establish medical science and art upon the only sure foundation, that of anatomy. May we not rightly speak of "the era of the Hunters," and associate the two brothers together in the great work they did for natural science?

EPOCH OF HUNTER'S DEATH.

Time will not admit of more than a brief allusion to the epoch of William Hunter's death in 1783. It was a period of great mental activity, and science was advancing with giant strides. Already his friend, Sir Joseph Banks, had entered upon his forty-two years' tenure of the chair of the Royal Society, where he was surrounded by a constellation of genius, every man taking rank as a discoverer of some great new fact or law in Nature. The modern science of chemistry was being rapidly evolved. Joseph Black, Cullen's pupil, had long discovered latent heat, Priestly had lately found oxygen ; Lavoisier was also at work, and air and water had just been resolved into their elements by Cavendish. The determination of colour vision by Dalton, and Rumford's investigations on heat followed soon after. Hunter's friend Franklin had discovered the properties of atmospheric electricity, and animal electricity and the nature of currents were now coming to light by the labours of Galvani and Volta ; but Faraday was yet unborn, and few of the secrets of this wonderful science had been revealed. Thomas Young and Wollaston, future leaders in physical science, were mere youths, and Humphry Davy was in the nursery. Mechanical applications of the laws of Nature were keeping pace with their discovery. Watt had already invented the steam-engine, and five years after Hunter's death it was applied to navigation by sea, whilst Erasmus Darwin, with the prescience of genius, was singing of its employment for locomotion on land. Herschell meanwhile was bringing to sight distant worlds and moons, by means of his giant refractors.

---

[1] Dr. John Brown, *Locke and Sydenham.*

Nor was it less an epoch of large political changes. The American colonies were separating themselves on the one hand, and on the other Governor Phillips was effecting the first settlement on the Australian continent. The French Revolution, like a dark cloud overhead, was about to burst with thunderclap upon astonished Europe. The year 1769, that year of momentous births, was passed, and had given to the world Bonaparte, and his Generals, Ney and Soult and Lannes; Mehemet Ali of Egypt, our own Wellington, Sydney Smith, Brunel, Humboldt, Sir Thomas Lawrence, and William Smith, the father of English geology.

The science upon which our own art is founded is in its turn built upon the physical sciences, and changes such as have been alluded to, influenced, more slowly perhaps, yet surely, the practice of medicine. The invention of the stethoscope by Laennec soon after this date revolutionised one department of medicine, as did later on the adaptation of the microscope to medical purposes, by the discoveries of Selligues and of J. J. Lister (father of Lord Lister).

The Brunonian system had its rise at this epoch, and lived its little day. Vaccination was discovered by William Hunter's pupil, Jenner, thirteen years after his death. The great Hunterian pupils, Abernethy and Astley Cooper, Anthony Carlisle, Cline and Clift, Macartney of Dublin, Physick of Philadelphia, were mostly boys at school. So were Henry Halford (Vaughan) and Charles Bell.

So full was the world of new thoughts and new knowledge, thus instinct with life and progress were the natural sciences, and such was the promise of the future, when the Hunters, who had done so much to lead men to the pure study of Nature, were passing away. Their work in biology had made the discoveries of others possible: for each generation, stepping on the shoulders of that which went before it, attains to heights that were as yet unknown. That we may not forget the great men who have gone before, but may remember how the precious heritage of our knowledge has been bought for us by the strenuous toil of giants in the past, is the purpose of orations such as this. And it is with that aim that I have brought before you this evening William Hunter, a man " by his life and by his art worthy of honour from all men to the end of time."—καὶ βίου καὶ τέχνης δοξαζομένος παρὰ πᾶσιν ἀνθρώποις εἰς τὸν ἀεὶ χρόνον.[1]

---

[1] Hippocrates, *Oath.*

THE HUNTERIAN MUSEUM, GLASGOW.

"Dr. W. Hunter's Collections were of extraordinary variety, considering the evidence that he took an active personal interest in every department. It is marvellous that he attained to such professional eminence while spreading his energies over so many fields.

"The illustrations of the 'Gravid Uterus' and of the Placenta are the most important in connection with his reputation as an obstetrician, and one of these has received his own sanction as specially worthy of attention, the specimen namely, which was introduced into the portrait by Sir Joshua Reynolds, painted to the commission of the University of Glasgow : it is injected and windowed so as to show the membranes through which the fœtus is visible.[1] The collection is essentially anatomical, including a large series of comparative preparations, made in connection with the *Zoological Department*, which is still steadily growing.

"This department, the central portion of the present collection, was, for the time and for a private museum, very large, and included a surprising variety of types, among others the Elephant, Giraffe, and Moose-deer. It is not possible now to identify the Hunterian Specimens as a whole, for apparently there were no labels on them when the museum was brought to Glasgow. But among the Invertebrates, in addition to a large series illustrating 'Conchology' in the old sense of the term, there are a

---

[1] The specimen is No. 158 of series forty-eight, in Dr. Teacher's *Catalogue*.

Pentacrinus, dilapidated as to the cup, and the type specimens of Ellis and Solander's work on the Corals, gathered on Cook's Transit Expedition, 1774.

"The *Minerals* which came from London are more distinctly recognisable, and an important series they were both scientifically and in point of value ; the collection is now trebled by the gifts of Eck and Dr. Brown of Lanfine. Among Hunter's papers occur brief notes of minerals indicating the care with which he gathered information regarding the specimens.   Mr. John Young, LL.D., Under-keeper to the Museum, has added to the Geological Section, so that it is now a valuable teaching collection in lithology, especially rich in the Carboniferous fossils.   The other formations are fairly represented.   The Pleistocene is rich from the work of D. Robertson, LL.D., Rev. Dr. H. W. Crosskey, and J. Young, LL.D.

"There was nothing corresponding to the modern meaning of *Ethnology*, but there is a very large assortment of weapons, implements etc., belonging to Cook's collections. Unlabelled as these were, identification with localities is impossible, except in the case of some which have been figured in the Narrative of the Voyages, as the Corals above mentioned in the monograph.

"Round an anatomist-physician's museum gathered an important *Bibliographic* collection, and this too was Hunter's personal care.   There are marked catalogues of book sales, letters from agents at home and abroad, all showing that Hunter selected what was bought.   The dealers' accounts were gone over carefully and checked. Large purchases were made in Paris and even Italy : volumes, sometimes series, came from monastic houses, or from private libraries, as those of Cæsar de Mussy, Colbert, etc., while a noble array of the Fathers bears the *fleur de lis* on the binding, but is only a part of the Royal property purchased.   Most of the important Continental and English presses are represented.   The Caxtons were recorded by Blades.   The Aldine Plato on vellum, bound by Derome in blue morocco, is perhaps the most exquisite book in the Library.   Alongside may be placed the vellum Greek Anthology, and the Vesalius, also on vellum, with the Titian plates, a work reproduced in facsimile by Stirling-Maxwell. A catalogue is now in course of preparation, and the section containing the fifteenth-century works, described by Rev. P. H. Aitken, has been made use of by Jenkinson in his recently published revision of Coppinger's additions to Hain. There is an interesting set of pamphlets regarding the North American Colonies, many concerning the time of Charles the first, and a whole library on the small-pox.

"The *Manuscripts* number over 600, excluding those which date from 1700 or thereby. The oldest is the Homilies of St. Basilius, A.D. 859. The Romaunt of the Rose, in French and in English, the Golden Legend, the Siege of Troy, the Canterbury Tales, Gower's Confessio Amantis and Vox Clamantis may be mentioned. Among illuminated MSS. are the Vita Christi, Boccaccio's Cas de Nobles Hommes et Femmes and the Cent Nouvelles Nouvelles. Bayer's Sinological MSS. have been catalogued and the list is published by Henri Cordier. A large number of the English manuscripts came from the Eastern Counties, Dr. Thomas Martin's autograph appearing on many of them. A list of this collection, not free from errors, is given by Haenel in his Catalogi Librorum MSS., but a new and more accurate catalogue is now in preparation, and nearly completed.

"The first Professor of Anatomy in the Royal Academy earned that position by his *artistic* proclivities as well as his reputation as an Anatomist. His diploma hangs in the Library, as does also a set of Engravings by Sir Robert Strange selected by the Engraver himself. There are many works in the Library selected obviously for their artistic contents. Thus Eisen, Gravelot, Moreau, Audran, etc., are well represented and there are three perfect copies of the Hypnerotomachia. Of the great Masters whose works adorn the Museum, Murillo, Rembrandt, De Koninck, Le Nain, Rubens, Salvator Rosa, Domenichino, Guido, Giordano, Charadin, Karl du Jardin, may be mentioned. Some of these were in Dr. Mead's collection and on his death acquired by Hunter. Among the Medical portraits are those of Vesalius by Titian, Mead and Charlton by Kneller, W. Hunter by Pine, Harvey by Bemmel, and Dr. Matthew Baillie. Kneller is also represented by the portrait of Sir Isaac Newton.

"The *Coin* cabinet is an extreme departure from the customary interests of a physician and anatomist. Yet the private papers show how unceasing was Hunter's care and how lavish his expenditure to make the collection complete. Part was catalogued by his friend Dr. C. Combe and published during Hunter's lifetime, in 1782, as the

Nummorum veterum Populorum et Urbium qui in Museo Gulielmi Hunter asservantur Descriptio, figuris illustrata, a work still spoken of with admiration for its accuracy. The munificence of a Glasgow merchant, Mr. James Stevenson, (Maecenas in respect of his Italian possessions,) has enabled a new edition of that catalogue to be undertaken, and the first volume, illustrated by collotypes, is now published. It is practically a new work, as Mr. George Macdonald, M.A., has included all the Colonial imperial pieces, as well as the whole of the British, Gaulish and Spanish Mints. But the republican money, the Imperial gold, silver and bronze greatly outnumber these, and the Western Empire is continued in a rich set of Papal and other Italian medals. The English and Scottish coinages are copiously represented, and there is a choice group of Renascence medals besides those in the Papal series. The whole collection numbers about 30,000 pieces." [1]

Dr. Combe's Catalogue " was far ahead of anything known at the time." For the first time, the weight, metal and size of every coin was stated. It was dedicated to the Queen, and the Latin preface states that upwards of £20,000 had been expended on the collection. A manuscript account by Dr. Hunter, preserved at Glasgow, accounts for more than £22,000. The Catalogue was to have extended over seven volumes, and the last of these, comprising the Saxon issues, had been committed to the Rev. R. Southgate. [2] The other volumes were to include (1) continuation of Dr. Combe's division, (2) money of Persia, Phœnicia, Samaria, Palmyra, Carthage, etc., (3) coins of the Kings, (4) Imperial coins struck in the Colonies and Greek cities, and (5) unpublished Roman coins. But all was interrupted by Hunter's death in 1783. [3]

The visitor should not omit to see the fine Armada medal, struck to commemorate the event and throwing a singular light on the feeling of the time. The Spanish ships with their great curved hulls are shown in a storm at sea, the scene being exquisitely moulded. On the reverse is seen a

---

[1] "The finest ever got together by a private individual" (Macdonald). The foregoing paragraphs have been kindly contributed by Professor John Young, M.D., the Keeper of the Museum, than whom no one can speak of its stores with more right or fuller knowledge.

[2] See *Gentleman's Magazine*, 1782, p. 519.

[3] See Mr. G. Macdonald's *Introduction to the Hunter Coin Cabinet, Stevenson Catalogue of Coins*, 1899, 4to, Vol. i. A Catalogue of duplicates was printed in 1777, 4to ; their sale occupied eight days, and realised £1,337. A second smaller sale followed in 1778.

semi-circle of popes, seated upon thrones, and kicking "against the pricks," in the shape of a forest of needles standing upright.[1]

The Museum was left, under the direction of Trustees, for the use of Hunter's nephew Matthew Baillie, in conjunction with Cruikshank, for the term of thirty years, and after that to the University of Glasgow. Cruikshank died in 1800, Baillie waived his right soon afterwards, and the Museum was removed in 1807. A fund of £8,000 was set apart in Hunter's will for the support and increase of the collection, and to promote its utility to the public, by means of lectures, etc., besides annuities of twenty pounds each to his three Trustees, Fordyce, Pitcairn and Combe, for thirty years.[2]

Dr. George Fordyce, F.R.S., (1736-1802) was physician to St. Thomas's Hospital, and long lectured on Chemistry and Materia Medica ; he took an important part in preparing the Pharmacopœia Londinensis. A rather eccentric man of rough exterior, he had original views on diet, subsisting himself upon one meal a day, taken punctually at four o'clock at Dolly's Chop-house in Paternoster Row. The meal consisted of a pound and a half of steak, a tankard of ale, a bottle of port wine, and a quarter of a pint of brandy. He died of gout.

Dr. David Pitcairn, F.R.S., (1749-1809) was nephew to Dr. William Pitcairn, of the "Currus triumphalis Opii." He was physician to St. Bartholomew's Hospital, and a man of much sagacity and high culture, with a fund of dry humour ; he was greatly mourned by his friends, when acute laryngitis ended his life.[3]

Dr. Charles Combe, F.R.S., (1743-1817) was of antiquarian tastes, and eminent as a collector of coins ; he also produced a famous edition of Horace. Dr. Combe took up Obstetric practice, and became physician to the British Lying-in

---

[1] The following exemplifies the free use of the Museum granted by Dr. Hunter to strangers : "On Monday every door of Dr. Hunter's Museum was opened to my leisure. His books, his medals, and his natural curiosities, which last are very numerous, and classed so well as to be of real use to any Naturalist." Rev. Michael Tyson to R. Gough. May 4, 1776. Nichols, *Literary Anecdotes*, VIII. 620.

[2] Hunter left £19,000 at his death. Besides the bequests just stated, he left an annuity of £100 to his sister Mrs. Baillie, and a sum of £2,000 to each of her two daughters. The residue, which was devised to Matthew Baillie, proved a very small one. "It was his intention," he told his nephew, "to leave him but little money, as he had derived too much pleasure from making his own fortune to deprive him of doing the same." See p. 27, and Wardrop's *Life of Baillie*. It is said that the Museum cost him £100,000.

[3] A letter to Baillie respecting the removal of the Museum is among the Hunter-Baillie MSS., vol. iii. p. 165.

Hospital.   He published an illustrated description of some
of the Hunter coins in 1782 as already mentioned, and he
made an effort after Hunter's death to keep the coins
permanently in London.[1]

The Hunterian Museum was at first housed in a handsome
Grecian temple built for the purpose, at a cost of £12,000, in
the gardens of the University in High Street, Glasgow.
Since the erection of the new University on Gilmore Hill in
1870, the Museum has been transferred thither, and is now
displayed in a series of fine rooms, where its treasures have
become better known, although scarcely yet as widely as
they deserve : the available space is already insufficient.
A general account of the Museum was published in 1813
by Captain Laskey.   No further Catalogue appeared until
1840, when a "Catalogue of the Anatomical Preparations"
was published.   The text of this was supplied by the
Manuscript Catalogue transmitted to the University long
before by the Trustees (and still in the Museum), which
bears the inscription : "The following Catalogue is, to the
best of our knowledge and belief, a true Catalogue of the
Anatomical Preparations left by the late Dr. William
Hunter.   (Signed) G. Fordyce, David Pitcairn, W. Combe."
The last survivor of these had been dead for more than
twenty years, but the custodians had collated the specimens
and corrected errors as far as they were able ; there were
many specimens missing, and many others undescribed.
The Catalogue formed a volume of 290 pages and was
divided into Sections.
No further catalogue of the Museum was, so far as appears,
issued until recent years.   Its contents have been more fully
studied by the present custodians, and excellent catalogues
of several departments have been published.   Professor
Young's address on the Library has been alluded to (see p.
11,) and a list of the Paintings and Engravings was
published by him some years ago.   Mr. Macdonald's
Catalogue of the Coin collection is noticed on a preceding
page.
A full and accurate Catalogue of the Anatomical and
Pathological Preparations has just been issued (1900) in two
volumes, by the liberal aid of the Bellahouston Trustees and
the indefatigable labours of Dr. J. H. Teacher.   The entire

----

[1] Dr. Teacher, *Introduction*, p. lxxiii.

series has been examined, the jars opened, and the objects and their descriptions as nearly as possible identified, with the help of all information that could be gleaned from Hunter's writings and other sources.

This department of the Museum consists of 2607 wet preparations preserved in jars, 19 large plaster of Paris casts, 410 bones, and 348 calculi and concretions. It is divided into eleven classes; that of Utero-gestation contains 271 specimens, including casts from the originals of Dr. Hunter's plates of the Gravid Uterus, and Placentæ showing the maternal and fœtal circulation. Upwards of one hundred of the plates in Dr. Baillie's "Series of Engravings to illustrate Morbid Anatomy," (London, 4to., 1803,) were taken from these preparations.

WILLIAM HUNTER'S WORKS.

[A list of the works will be found at the end of this chapter.]

William Hunter's greatest work is the *Anatomy of the Human Gravid Uterus*, which has been already described,[1] and which was published in 1774, and again in 1815. Two of the smaller plates were reproduced by Hogben in his "Anatomical Tables of Midwifery" in 1811, and Hunter's entire work was re-issued, from the original copper-plates, very little worn, by the Sydenham Society, in 1851. This work has ever been highly valued on the continent of Europe as well as in our own country. Soemmering published in his "Icones Embryonum humanorum," in 1799, two plates of the human embryo, which should form, as he said, a supplement to those of Hunter, to whom he refers as "Vir ille summus, fautor noster insignis." Hunter's plates were all or most of them copied by Loder in his "Tabulae Anatomicae" (Vimariae, 1803), but the execution is inferior and the size generally reduced. To the names of the German Biologist and the St. Petersburg Professor may be added that of a renowned Italian. Caldani, the physiologist, crowned his many works by the issue in his old age of four magnificent volumes, "Icones Anatomicae."[2] In these he included the whole of Hunter's plates, which form Nos. 135 to 167 of the series, but although the engraving is excellent, the work of the Italian artists (Zuliani and Ambrosi) does not come up to that of Rymsdyk[3]

---

[1] See p. 18.

[2] Venice, 1801-1813, elephant folio.

[3] This artist spelt his name indifferently, J. Van Rymsdyk, Riemsdyk, and Reimsdyk.

in Hunter's original volume. The delicacy and softness of the latter bespeak a labour of love, in which neither time nor cost were an object, and they are only equalled by William Clift's drawing of the placenta of a monkey to illustrate the works of John Hunter.

In 1794, eleven years after Hunter's death, appeared *An Anatomical Description of the Human Gravid Uterus and its Contents*, the text of which had been left in manuscript by Hunter, and was now published by his nephew, Dr. Matthew Baillie, with a few corrections, and the addition of some pages at the end. A second edition was issued by Dr. E. Rigby in 1843. The part contributed by Baillie contains the mistaken account of the origin of the Decidua which has been already alluded to. [1] One sentence from this treatise was much quoted by Dr. Robert Lee in his controversy (1839-1848) on the nerves of the uterus. It is as follows : "I cannot take upon me to say what change happens to the system of uterine nerves from utero-gestation, but I suspect them to be enlarged in some proportion as the vessels are." This sentence is a good example of Hunterian *dicta* : for it betokens a wide view of the subject, which left nothing out, a judicial temper, which stated nothing as a fact that observation had not first proved, and lastly a faculty of insight, leading to shrewd opinion, which might wait perhaps a century for its verification. Dr. Lee, who by the way omitted the word ' some ' near the end of the sentence, maintained stoutly against all critics that the nerves of the uterus were enlarged during pregnancy. Astley Cooper called his preparations "cart ropes and chain-cables," and it was several years before the heat of the controversy died down, but Lee's views received in the end a considerable measure of acceptance. [2]

William Hunter is sometimes alluded to as one of the pioneers of Ovariotomy, but this credit belongs probably less to him than to Pott and to Blundell. His observations on the extirpation of diseased ovaries occur in the admirable Remarks on the Cellular Membrane and on Dropsies which were appended to his paper on Emphysema read in 1757. [3] "It has been proposed indeed, " he says, "by modern

[1] See p. 18.
[2] Dr. Alexander Morison has lately revived the subject, and published some observations which favour the opposite view, which was John Hunter's. *Lancet*, 1898, vol ii. p. 1612.
[3] *Med. Obs. and Inquiries.* See List of Works, and p. 22.

Surgeons, deservedly of the first reputation, to attempt a radical cure by incision and suppuration, or by the excision of the cyst." He goes on to discuss the nature of the ovarian cyst, "as it has appeared to me in a number of cases both in the living and dead body." He concludes by pointing out the great and almost overwhelming dangers of the operation ; but concludes : "surely, in a case otherwise so desperate, it might be adviseable to do it, could we know beforehand that the circumstances would admit of such treatment."

Dr. Hunter's paper on the Sigaultean operation for *Division of the Symphysis Pubis* is dated 1778, and was published as a supplement to a treatise by Dr. Vaughan of Leicester. [1] This operation had just been introduced with great *éclat* by eminent surgeons in France. Dr. Hunter writes in a philosophical spirit. He deprecates desperate operations undertaken on a bare chance of saving life, and declares that the life of the mother is of incomparably greater value than that of an unborn child. He questions the wisdom of the early approbation of a new practice by an authoritative body such as the Faculty of Medicine at Paris. He illustrates the question of new methods by the use of the forceps, which, though it was sometimes of service, and might save either the mother or child, and had been sometimes used by him with advantage, yet "I am clearly of opinion . . . that the forceps (midwifery instruments in general I fear), upon the whole, has done more harm than good." With regard to the operation itself, he had had occasion to perform it often upon dead bodies, and found that an adequate separation of the bones required much wrenching, and that the (sacro-iliac) ligaments at the back of the pelvis were torn. He then showed from actual examination of some contracted pelves for which the Cæsarian section had been used, that the contraction was such that no division of the symphysis could have permitted a child to pass.

Was the operation advisable to save the child in certain difficult labours, where the crotchet was now used ? He preferred the crotchet because it was safer for the mothers, and gave less suffering than "to have the strongest joints of their body cut and torn asunder, to secure a *chance* only of a living child ." Yet he thought the section of the Symphysis

---

[1] It was read before the "Medical Society of Physicians" but never published in the *Medical Observations*, although Osborn (footnote to p. 318 of his *Essays on Midwifery*) states otherwise.

might possibly be found better than the Cæsarian section in a very few rare cases,—to save the mother's life ; cases of very narrow pelvis, or great projection of the spine, so that the crotchet could not be used until division of the symphysis had made room for it. Such an operation, and indeed all operative measures in midwifery, should only be used after due "consultation and formality." Osborn, in 1792, argues at length against Hunter's admission, guarded though it is, of Symphysiotomy as a possible resource under any conditions, and the operation, though it has found some supporters since that day, has been generally abandoned.

On the discovery by the Hunters of the placental structure and circulation, reference may be made to John Hunter's paper (not published by the Royal Society on account of the dispute with his brother as to priority), which is contained in his collected Works.[1] A critique upon it is added by Professor Owen, dealing with Dr. Lee's opinions in opposition to the Hunters' doctrine, and relating experiments of his own which confirm it. Dr. Horrocks, in the Hunterian Society's Oration for 1898, quotes W. Hunter's description of the Placenta, and places it side by side with the most recent exposition of its anatomy by Leopold of Dresden, showing their agreement in essential features. The dispute between the brothers arose, if we are to believe Jesse Foot, about a morbid specimen which John invited William to see, and which William carried off for his Museum. But perhaps there was never a work of more singular scandal and malignity than Foot's "Life of John Hunter," published under the cloak of an honourable love of truth, and pursuing its victim in his new-made grave. "John Hunter," he says, "never was the author of any production which appeared under his name" : Smollett wrote them for him. His plate of the Placenta "gives just as good an idea of the country in the *moon* as it does of that which it is intended to explain :—it will serve for either." [2]

W. Hunter's paper *On the Uncertainty of the signs of Murder in the case of Bastard Children*, alluded to on page 23, long occupied an important place in the field of Legal

---

[1] Ed. Palmer, vol. iv. p. 60. See above, pp. 13, 17.

[2] Foot, *Life of John Hunter*, pp 62, 222. Foot's illwill may have been in part an expression of that prejudice against the Hunters as Scotchmen, which according to Agnes Baillie was very rife in their lifetime and afterwards. See her notes on the Pedigree of the Hunters, *Hunter-Baillie MSS.* Compare Horace Walpole's anecdote, quoted on another page.

Medicine. Its reprint by Dr. Samuel Farr in 1815 has been already mentioned, and in the same year it was appended to the third English edition of Faselius' "Elements of Medical Jurisprudence." The paper was also separately published in 1818, and it has been translated into at least one European language.[1] Dr. William Cummin in 1836 included it in his little volume on "The Proofs of Infanticide," and he writes of it, fifty-three years after Hunter's death, as "the most influential and popular tract on Child-murder hitherto produced in this country." "The judges quote it," he continues, "with implicit faith in its perfection : the bar study it, and cross-examine the crown witnesses on the difficulties which it suggests ; and medical men probably will not find it safe to venture into the witness-box without being familiarly acquainted with its contents." Dr. Cummin, however, sets himself to controvert the author's positions, and especially the objections which Hunter felt to the certainty of the test of the lungs floating in water, as a sign that the child had lived. Hunter's paper has often been quoted since by writers on Medical Jurisprudence, and although it was obviously written for a special purpose,—to show the uncertainty of signs which at that day were regarded as infallible proofs of guilt, and of guilt meriting the penalty of death, and therefore it partakes slightly of a partisan spirit ; yet it is a masterly exposition of its subject, and still worthy of careful study by those who would know all the considerations which must be taken into account, in judging of the actions of women under the dreadful conditions of illegitimate childbirth.

Dr. Gooch, in his "Practical Compendium of Midwifery," 1831, refers to W. Hunter's observations on rabbits, as having confirmed and given general credence in this country to De Graaf's discovery of the descent of the ovum through the Fallopian tube. Hunter's experience in a case in which the production of abortion was attempted at the third month of pregnancy is also referred to.[2]

Darwin has preserved a notable instance of Hunter's practice of testing received opinions. On the belief that the imagination of the mother affects the child *in utero*, he writes :

---

[1] An Italian translation is included in the second volume of the *Raccolta di Trattati e memorie di legislazione e giurisprudenza criminale.* Firenze, 1821, 1822.

[2] Gooch, pp. 78, 92.

" Dr. William Hunter, in the last century, told my father [1] that during many years every woman in a large London Lying-in Hospital was asked before her confinement whether anything had specially affected her mind, and the answer was written down ; and it so happened that in no one instance could a coincidence be detected between the woman's answer and any abnormal structure ; but when she knew the nature of the structure, she frequently suggested some fresh cause." [2]

Smellie and William Hunter stand at the head of the line of British leaders in Obstetric Medicine. After their day came Denman,[3] whose daughter Matthew Baillie married, and who was father to Lord Chief-Justice Denman ; and after him Osborn, Haighton, Merriman, Gooch, Blundell, Ramsbotham and many others. In Blundell's portrait, by Room, one may read, amongst the volumes which adorn his bookshelves, the title, " W. Hunter's Works."

Dr. Hunter's *Medical Commentaries*, Part I., issued in 1762, was intended as the first of a series of similar works. It deals with physiological topics,—of the injection of the tubes of the testis and epididymis with mercury ; of the lymphatic vessels, previously accounted to be blood-vessels, and of their function as absorbents like the lacteals[4] ; of transudation from veins, and whether they absorb as well ; of the vessels of cartilage, where the author confesses a mistaken observation in his first paper before the Royal Society ; of the discovery of the ducts of the lachrymal gland ; of the membrana pupillaris ; of the insensibility of tendons and Haller's views thereon (there was no dispute with him) ; and of what is now called congenital hernia.

In most of these subjects Dr. Hunter had made discoveries, some of much importance—discoveries described in his lectures, which, unlike those of Cullen, were never printed. In these researches he had sometimes been anticipated by others, for there were working in Europe at this time not a few keen and able anatomists. Much material too, in the

---

[1] Grandfather (?). Charles Darwin's father was born seventeen years only before Hunter's death.
[2] *The Variation of Animals and Plants*, vol i., p. 264.
[3] Denman dedicated the first two editions of his *Essay on the Puerperal Fever* to W. Hunter.
[4] At p. 58 is recorded a curious case of lymphatic fistula in the groin, the closure of which was followed by lymphatic œdema of the whole limb, which ultimately subsided. Sografi expounded Hunter's doctrines, a few years later : *Exercitatio anatomico-chirurgica . . . . in qua theoria lymphæ ductuum ex observationibus Hunteri, Monroi et propriis exponitur.* Patavii, 1766.

volume, was derived from John Hunter's labours, and this is generously acknowledged by his brother. But Dr. Hunter was most unfortunate in his manner of presenting his claims to the world. His *Commentaries* are couched in a style of address that has happily become extinct in these days, jealousy for his own fame leading him into bitter controversy with other workers in the same field, so that it is hardly to be regretted that, beyond a supplement added in 1764, containing his dispute with Pott, no further parts of these *Commentaries* were ever issued, for the style increases in acerbity to the very last pages of the supplement. It is said that Smollett revised the work after Hunter had written it; perhaps the sharpest arrows were barbed by the author of *Peregrine Pickle*.[1]

His principal antagonists in controversy were Alexander Monro, father and son. Alexander Monro Secundus was a younger man than his opponent, whose lectures he at one time attended, and he lived on to the enjoyment of an old age not granted to the Hunters. The great Edinburgh anatomist's treatises between 1758 and 1762 are full of controversy with Hunter, with Hewson, and with Akenside, pursued in a like ungenerous spirit, though his pen is not quite so trenchant as Hunter's.[2] When Monro's Memoir and collected essays were published under the filial care of Monro Tertius in 1840 the dust of the war of pens had long been laid, and little reference is made to its heat and bitterness. The disputes "may have had their use by rousing the energies of both parties," but it now matters little whether the one or the other were first in the field; each did noble work in adding to the store of knowledge.

Percival Pott was five years Hunter's senior. He replied to the strictures contained in the *Commentaries*, but did not descend to use the tone adopted by his antagonist.[3]

A singular illustration (probably authentic) of Hunter's bitter tongue and pen is preserved at the Royal College of Surgeons. It is a facsimile letter appended to a black and

---

[1] Smollett's part in it is well known, according to Dr. Teacher *(Introduction to Catalogue)*. Simmons calls the style "correct and spirited!" A second edition was published in 1777, apparently without any change.

[2] See *Observations, . . . wherein Dr. Hunter's Claim to some Discoveries is examined.* By A. Monro, Jun., M.D., Edinburgh, 1758. *An Expostulatory Epistle* to Hunter was published in 1762.

[3] Pott's *Works*, by Earle, new edition, 1808, Vol. I., p. xvi.; Vol. II., p. 115, footnote. Another critic was Dr. J. Garner, whose *Observations on Dr. Hunter's Medical Commentaries* are noticed adversely in the *Critical Review*, Jan. 1763, p. 70.

white caricature portrait (noticed on another page) and runs as follows : " Dr. Hunter is sorry that Mr. Da Costa has taken so much trouble. It is a thing of very little conse-quence, but cannot be set right because it was very wrong. Mr. Dacosta's owning that it was wrong is enough. But it must remain so. Dr. Hunter chuses no further dealings.— He thinks Mr. Drury likewise has behaved in a way which he should not have expected. But if they are pleased with themselves he has nothing to say. N.B. 10 January 1771."[1]

Perhaps no treatment received by Hunter would fully justify such an epistle. Yet we are not to conclude that he was a proud supercilious man, insensible to nobler feelings. The fast friend of the gentle Fothergill, the chosen inter-mediary in a difficult mission with Hume, the physician who won the Queen's warm regard, who enjoyed a life-long fellowship with men like Cullen and Pitcairn, and whose high sense of duty led him to spend the strength of a life-time in teaching to others all he knew, his was no mean or selfish nature. A sensitive mind, too conscious of its own power and rights, a lonely heart, unsoftened by domestic love, these left Hunter sometimes the prey of resentments which were ill-natured and bitter. They brought their own Nemesis, for they lessened the sum of his happiness.

Two Introductory Lectures to Dr. Hunter's last course of Anatomical Lectures at his Theatre in Windmill Street were printed by order of the Trustees in 1784, the year after his death, as they were left corrected for the Press by himself.[2]

In the first lecture Dr. Hunter traces the origin of Ana-tomical study in early ages, and gives an account of Aristotle and Galen, filling in the outline of history in such a way as shows him to be no mean student. After Galen anatomy declined, and Hunter remarks here that when any man has " carried his art far beyond all others, it seems to throw the rest of the world into a kind of despair." Hopeless of im-proving the art further, men do nothing, and in course of time deify the great man, so that every page of his writings

---

[1] The letter refers without doubt to the collecting of natural history specimens for Hunter's Museum, a frequent source of contentions. Da Costa was a naturalist, especially learned on fossils, a Jew by race. Unhappily his methods were far from straight, and he was, I believe, in prison when this letter was written. Fothergill and Pulteney still helped him in his troubles, and he attained fame afterwards as an author. Dru Drury was an eager entomologist and a very upright man.

[2] The date of his revision seems to have been about 1776 ; see p. 58 of the Lectures.

becomes infallible. "Such respect," he adds, "must always
be a mark of declining science."[1] In the long period of
Arabian supremacy it was still translations from Galen that
ruled anatomical science, until the period of the Renaissance.
Here Hunter shows a keen sense of how much we owe to
Greek learning. He speaks very highly of Leonardo da
Vinci as an anatomist, and hopes to engrave and publish his
designs.

Here also is to be found Hunter's estimation of Harvey,
whom he places at a less exalted level than others had done,
and defends his position by argument drawn from a careful
study of the subject. The history of the Science is traced to
his own time, with notices of Albinus, Douglas and others
who had been his masters, as well as John Hunter, Hewson
and Cruikshank, all of whom he had "bred to Anatomy."

Hunter took no mean view of his art. The second lecture
opens with words from Fontenelle and from Cicero, to show
how the order and beauty of the human frame reveal a
divine intelligence.[2] Who can consider these proofs, he
goes on, without longing for another life after this, when we
may see and comprehend the whole plan of the Creator in
forming the Universe and directing its operations ? Then he
passes to the use of Anatomy, and lays down doctrines which
have become in our day the foundation stones of medical
science. The study of the body in health must be the direct
road to the knowledge of disease. By an intimate acquaintance with the economy of our bodies we may discover even
the seeds of disease. Anatomy is the basis not only of
Surgery but of Medicine. Who are they, he cries, who
"would persuade students that a little of Anatomy is enough
for a physician, and a little more too much for a surgeon ?
God help them : They have it not themselves, and are afraid
that others should get it." His foresight told him that the
most probable future improvements in physic "would arise
from a more general, and more accurate examination of
disease after death."

Going on to unfold the science of Anatomy by analytical
and synthetical methods, he speaks with just pride of his
own part. "I have collected such an anatomical apparatus

---

[1] The present author's copy of the *Lectures* contains at this point the quaint marginal
note in pencil, dated, it will be observed, the year after John Hunter died ; "Amen. 1794.
Scripsit hoc the Devil."

[2] The like thought finds expression in the writings of a medical seer, whose wise and
gentle spirit has hardly yet found fitting reverence amongst us, the late Dr. H. G. Sutton.
Preface to *Lectures on Medical Pathology*, 1886.

as was never brought together in any age or country." He himself continued his lectures from a sense of public duty. It appears that more than twenty years before his death Dr. Hunter felt compelled by pressure of other work, and privation of natural rest, to give up his lectures, but his hearers pressed upon him so earnestly to continue them, that on deliberate reflection he thought it his duty to do so even at much loss to himself. " He conceived that a man may do infinitely more good to the public by teaching his art, than by practising it. The good effects of the latter must center in the advantage of the few individuals that may be under his care as patients ; but the influence of a teacher extends itself to the whole nation, and descends to posterity." [1] These words breathe a noble spirit, and are worthy of the man who set duty before fame or riches or the claims of old age, and, when all these were his, rose from his last sick-bed to lecture to his waiting students. Such a man was not only a great Teacher, but a maker of Teachers for the generation to come,—the leaders of Anatomical Science both in England and America.[2]

Pursuing his theme, Hunter avows his own ignorance of many questions relating to animal operations ; such as sensation, motion, respiration, digestion etc. " In my opinion all these subjects are much less understood than most people think them." The sects of Physiologists had sought to explain the functions on totally different principles. "Some have made the stomach a mill ; some would have it to be a stewing-pot ; and some a wort-trough : yet all the while, one would have thought that it must have been very evident, that the stomach was neither a mill, nor a stewing-pot, nor a wort-trough, nor anything but a stomach." Mechanical and chemical visions had taken the place of observations. His own practice in teaching physiology was to lay before his students the structure of parts and the known phenomena, as *data* ; to state the prevailing opinions, with the chief arguments on either side ; and then sometimes to give his own opinion with caution, " but more generally to leave your

---

[1] *Memorial* to the Earl of Bute, appended to *Introductory Lectures*, p. 120.

[2] As Physick, the famous pupil of John Hunter, became in 1805 the first Professor of Surgery proper in the University of Philadelphia, so at an earlier date, William Shippen, jun., inaugurated the Professorship of Anatomy and Surgery in that University in 1765. Shippen was an enthusiastic pupil of W. Hunter, and an admirable lecturer, forming himself after Hunter's model. See Dr. J. Carson's *History of the Medical Department of the University of Pennsylvania*. Philadelphia, 1869; also a letter from Dr. Shippen to W. Hunter in the *Introduction* to Dr. Teacher's *Catalogue*, p. xxv., footnote.

judgements free, that enquiry and improvement may go on."
He never aimed at displaying his own knowledge, but
laboured to show what the students ought to know.   This
excluded all declamation, parade, wrangling, subtlety.   Time
and labour were not spared.   He lectured for two hours,
from two to four o'clock every day, except Sunday, and the
course lasted nearly four months.   He closes with some good
advice to students, about the taking of notes, and their plan
of study and dissection, showing how earnest was his desire,
by teaching openly all he knew, to train them to observe for
themselves, and so to give them no mere cram knowledge,
but that which should be impressed on their minds, by
strong and clear conceptions of things that had been under
the examination of their own senses.   The man who so
taught for nearly forty years may have been in truth "the
best teacher of Anatomy that ever lived." [1]

It has been already noted [2] that the first lecture of the
course was of a more general character, and that it was open
to the attendance of others besides the students.   Horace
Walpole relates an amusing instance of the latitude which the
lecturer sometimes allowed himself.   "Dr. Hunter," he
writes, in October 1780, "had the impudence t'other day to
pour out at his Anatomic lecture a more outrageous Smeltiad
than Smelt himself, and imputed all our disgraces and ruin
to the Opposition.   Burke was present, and said he had
heard of Political Arithmetic, but never before of Political
Anatomy." [3]

Papers relating to Dr. Hunter's intended *Plan for
establishing a Museum in London* for the Improvement of
Anatomy, Surgery, and Physic, were printed with the
Introductory Lectures.   They include, a Memorial to Lord
Bute ; Plan of a Theatre, Museum etc., with an account of
plots of land in Westminster, 1764 ; a memorandum given to
the King by Mr. Hawkins ; and Hunter's final letter to the
Right Honourable George Grenville, ending the matter.

---

[1] See page 20. He describes the ingenious construction of his theatre at Windmill Street,
in which the tiers of seats rose circularly around the demonstrating table, which was placed
midway between the centre of the room and its circumference. *Introd. Lectures*, p. 111.
It would seem from an allusion in his *Commentaries* (Supplement, p. 20) that he had an
audience of about 100 ; this was in 1756. Hunter's pioneer work, in the first establishment
of complete courses of Anatomical Lectures and dissections in England is acknowledged in
the *Report from the Select Committee on Anatomy, 1828, to the House of Commons.*
[2] See p. 15.
[3] Walpole's *Letters*, Ed. 1857, vii. 456. Walpole in his bantering way calls Hunter " that
Scotch nightman," and says he might teach the youngest Prince his Erse Alphabet, but
other references show that they were on terms of friendship.

This scheme, dear to the Anatomist's heart, has been already described (see page 11) ; its failure doubtless moved him to bequeath his own Museum away from London. The comparative neglect of this Museum, and of John Hunter's, for a generation or more after the death of the founders, shows how little their true value was known to the men of their own day. In later times both Museums have been highly prized.

William Hunter's papers upon medical and surgical topics contributed to the "Medical Observations and Inquiries" have been already noticed (see pages 21 to 23), and a complete list of them will be found at the end of this chapter. According to Waldeyer a number of these papers were translated into German and published at Leipzig soon after Hunter's death.[1]

Before the Royal Society Hunter read seven papers. The first was in 1743 upon *Articulating Cartilages* (see page 8). Twenty-five years elapsed before his next communication, in 1768, entitled, *Observations on the bones, commonly supposed to be Elephant's bones, which have been found near the river Ohio in America.* He discusses the origin of these fossil bones with the keen interest of a geologist. A short paper in 1770 gave an *Account of some bones found in the rock of Gibraltar,* encrusted with calcareous matter ; and in the same year he contributed an *Account of the Nyl-ghau, an Indian animal, not hitherto described.* This was illustrated by a good figure, and a systematic description of the bodily structure and functions of the animal.

In 1774 or 1775 he read an essay *On the Origin of the Venereal Disease.* In this paper he opposed the view of Astruc that Syphilis was brought into Europe by Columbus on his first expedition. But the testimony of Peter Martyr to the previous existence of the disease in Spain did not on fuller research satisfy his mind, and the paper was never published.

The last of Hunter's papers before the Royal Society was read in 1777, and gives *A short account of the late Dr. Maty's illness.* The disease appears to have been Stricture of the Colon.

A new method of the administration of mercury in Syphilis by rubbing calomel into the mucous membrane of

---

[1] Waldeyer, *Biographisches Lexikon der Aertzte*, 1886, Art. 'W. Hunter.' The papers were published by Kuhn in two volumes 8vo. in 1784-5 (Dr. Teacher).

the lips and mouth, had been devised by Mr. Peter Clare.[1]
Dr. Hunter wrote in support of it, pointing out the absorp-
tion of substances, especially in a watery medium, from all
mucous surfaces, and deeming that when gradually absorbed
from the surface of the mouth the mercury would be less
irritating to the digestive tract lower down than if swallowed.
Clare speaks in his paper in the warmest terms of Hunter as
his teacher.

Mention may here be made of two pamphlets, in which
Hunter was attacked by a young medical *confrère*, Dr.
William Rowley, a man of no high reputation, but of a very
active pen, writing medical treatises for popular reading.
" A letter to Dr. William Hunter, on the dangerous tendency
of medical vanity, occasioned by the death of the late Lady
Holland," appeared in 1774 ; and in the following year, " A
second letter to Dr. William Hunter, being an answer to the
liberal criticism in the *Monthly Review* for November, 1774,
. . . and some account of the new-discovered methods
of curing schirrus breasts without cutting, the cancer, ulcers
of the uterus, the scrophula, ulcers of the legs, and restoring
sight to the blind, by internal medicines only."

The burden of Rowley's complaint was that Hunter had
prevented his attendance on Lady Holland, who had died of
cancer under Hunter's care, and that the latter used hemlock[2] and opium, drugs which Rowley deemed worthless in
such disorders. Other cases of cancer are related, some of
which, according to Rowley's claim, were cured by his
treatment. Perhaps the chief interest now attaches to a
series of prescriptions which are quoted, with the joint
signatures of Fothergill and Hunter, met in consultation
over one of these cases. Few copies of Rowley's pamphlets
now exist ; perhaps not more than one copy of each in this
country.[3]

---

[1] *An Essay on the cure of Abscesses by caustic . . . also a new method of curing
the Lues Venerea, etc., with the remarks of Dr. Hunter, etc.* 2nd Edition. Lond., 1779.
A third editon appeared next year.

[2] The hemlock, then called *Cicuta*, was at this time much used, Baron Störck having
brought it into repute in 1760 as a cure for cancer and other chronic maladies. Fothergill,
Rutty and others employed it largely ; Cullen, however, in 1789 gives a very qualified
account of its value, and its use afterwards became limited to its narcotic applications.
From the 1898 British Pharmacopœia all the preparations of hemlock have gone, excepting
the *Succus* and the Tincture.

[3] A copy of the first is in the Library of the Royal Medical and Chirurgical Society,
London ; and one of the second is in the Bodleian Library, Oxford. Both are in the Library
of the Surgeon-General at Washington, U.S.A., and my thanks are due to Dr. J. C. Merrill,
the Librarian, for his courtesy in sending me a *précis* of the second letter. Inquiry has
failed to reveal the existence of any other copies.

At the end of a fine copy[1] of Hunter's lectures, written down in manuscript by one of his pupils, is a lecture on *The Art of Embalming dead Bodies*, delivered January 13th, 1776. In this he enters in much detail into the subject, expounds his reasonings and observations upon it, and describes a process which he had devised and used in several cases. He relied much on the injection of turpentine compounded with other substances, and subsequently laying the embalmed body in Plaster of Paris. But the art was not to be exercised without great labour, so that he concludes, " considering the trouble you must have during all these Processes now laid down you ought not to undertake it under 100 guineas."

Amongst other works which Dr. Hunter had planned, but did not live to execute, were a systematic account of the *Lymphatic System*, and a treatise on *Calculi* and Concretions. The former was issued three years after his death by his partner and assistant, W. Cruikshank, who quotes freely from the discoveries and work of Hunter. For the latter he had made a rich collection of specimens, which are in the Hunterian Museum in Glasgow, together with a set of twenty-one finely wrought plates, containing 104 figures.

Some of his medical manuscripts are preserved in his Museum ; amongst them are critical notes of lectures attended by him when a young man,—those of Ferrein in Paris in 1743-4, and those of S. Sharpe of Guy's Hospital in 1746. There is also a diary of his attendance upon Queen Charlotte commencing in 1762, and including three confinements.[2]

Manuscript notes of Hunter's Lectures, taken down by his pupils, are to be found in several medical libraries. In London, that of the Royal College of Surgeons is exceptionally rich in manuscript copies of these lectures, of which a critical catalogue has been made by Dr. Teacher : some are of great interest. Other excellent copies are in the Library of the Royal Medical and Chirurgical Society, and some in those of the Royal Colleges of Physicians, both in London and Edinburgh.

These notes on William Hunter's works may be fitly concluded by a passage from his last written introductory lecture (p. 92) :—" Every man should be held as a criminal who locks up his talent, whatever it may be. Mine, from nature, was small ; but by application and perseverance it has grown to be considerable."

Royal Coll. Surg. England. 42. c. 35. ᵃ See p. 9, and Dr. J. H. Teacher's *Lecture*.

LIST OF WILLIAM HUNTER'S WORKS.

(A) PUBLISHED WORKS.

I. Medical Commentaries. Part 1. Containing a plain and direct answer to Prof. Monro, jun., interspersed with Remarks on the Structure, Functions, and Diseases of several parts of the Human Body. London, 1762. (Four fine plates by Riemsdyk. 113 pp. 4to., including an Appendix).

II. A Supplement to the First Part of the Medical Commentaries. London, 1764. (33 pp. 4to.)

III. The Anatomy of the Human Gravid Uterus exhibited in figures. Birmingham, John Baskerville, 1774. (34 Plates, some of them 23 by 17 inches, the figures mostly of life size, with Preface and descriptions in Latin and English, in parallel columns : the Latin version of the Preface was corrected by Sir George Baker, Bart. Large Folio. Price at issue, six guineas.)

IV. Reflections on dividing the Symphysis of the Ossa Pubis. (Published as a Supplement to the 2nd Edition of Dr. J. Vaughan's " Cases and Observations on the Hydrophobia, etc., London." Preface dated 1778).

V. Two Introductory Lectures, delivered by Dr. William Hunter, to his last course of Anatomical Lectures, at his Theatre in Windmill Street : as they were left corrected for the Press by himself.

To which are added some Papers relating to Dr. Hunter's intended Plan for establishing a Museum in London, for the improvement of Anatomy, Surgery, and Physic. Printed by Order of the Trustees, London, 1784. (130 pp. 4to.)

VI. An Anatomical Description of the Human Gravid Uterus, and its contents. London 1794. (88 pp. 4to. Edited by Baillie, who supplied the latter pages in completion of the work).

(See also, Remarks on the administration of mercury, appended to Mr. Clare's Essay, noticed on a former page.)

(B) PAPERS READ BEFORE THE ROYAL SOCIETY.

See *Philosophical Transactions*, volumes 42nd to 69th.

I. On the Structure and Diseases of Articulating Cartilages. 1743

II. Observations on the bones, commonly supposed to be Elephants' bones, which have been found near the river Ohio in America. 1768

III. Account of some bones found in the rock of Gibraltar. 1770

IV. An Account of the Nyl-ghau, an Indian animal, not hitherto described. 1770

V. Account of the fusing of a Bell-wire by Lightning. (Not published[1]). 1772

VI. On the Origin of the Venereal Disease. (Not published). 1774 or 1775

VII. A short account of the late Dr. Maty's illness. (In conjunction with Mr. H. Watson). 1777

Besides these papers Hunter communicated a paper by Hewson, at that time working in his dissecting room, on the Lymphatic System in Birds, in which Hunter's own discoveries are referred to. 1768

---

[1] The MS. of this short paper is in Hunter's Museum (Teacher).

Also Dr. Fordyce and Mr. Alchorne reported "An
Examination of various Ores in the Museum
of Dr. William Hunter."   1779

(C)   PAPERS READ BEFORE THE "MEDICAL
SOCIETY OF PHYSICIANS,"

and published in its *Medical Observations and
Inquiries.* (Six volumes, 1757 to 1784.)

I. The History of an Aneurysm of the Aorta,
with some remarks on Aneurysms in
general. (2 large plates.) (Vol. i., p. 323.)   1757(?)

II. The History of an Emphysema, followed
by Remarks on the Cellular membrane
and some of its diseases. (A long and
very instructive paper.) (Vol. ii., p. 17.)   1757

III. Account of a diseased Tibia as a Supplement to the last article, (*i.e.*, to Dr.
Mackenzie's account of separation of
part of the thigh bone.) (2 plates.)
(Vol. ii., p. 303.)   1761

IV. Remarks on the Symphysis of the Ossa
Pubis. (Vol. ii., p. 333.)   1761

V. Further observations upon a particular
species of Aneurysm. (Arterio-venous
Aneurysm was now first described.)
(Vol. ii., p. 390.)   1761

VI. Introduction to Mr. Teckel's paper on the
Insensibility of Tendons. (Vol. iv., p.
343.)   1770

VII. Postscript to Mr. Armiger's letter on the
Varicose Aneurysm. (Vol. iv., p. 385.)   1770(?)

VIII. Appendix to Mr. John Lynn's "History of
a fatal Inversion (Retroversion) of the
(gravid) Uterus."   (Vol. iv., p. 400.)   1770(?)

IX. Summary Remarks on the Retroverted
Uterus. (Vol. v., p. 388.)   1775(?)

X. On the Uncertainty of the Signs of Murder, in the Case of Bastard Children. (Long and admirably reasoned ; this paper was published in 1818 in a separate form.) (Vol. vi., p. 266.)   1783

XI. Three cases of Mal-conformation in the Heart. (With remarks containing some of the essentials of the doctrine of evolution.) (Vol. vi., p. 291.)   1783

XII. The successful Cure of a severe Disorder of the Stomach by Milk taken in small Quantities at once. (With a letter from Mr. Wm. Hey, as an appendix, relating four additional cases.) (Vol. vi., p. 310.)   1783

(The three latter papers, upon which alone the reputation of a medical philosopher and clinician might well be established, were not read before the Society until after the author's death. Various other papers by surgeons and country physicians were communicated to the Society by W. Hunter. Mention may here also be made of a letter from Dr. A. Hunter, of York, to Dr. W. Hunter, giving an account of the cure of a case of severe hydrocephalus by repeated vapour-baths ; see *Med. Comment.* (Duncan), viii., p. 106. Mr. R. Bayley, a surgeon, published at New York, about 1781, a series of cases of Angina Trachealis, in a letter to W. Hunter. Lastly, Dr. Anthony Fothergill read before the Medical Society of London in 1786, an account of a case of enlarged Prostate Gland, and quoted a short but excellent letter from Dr. Hunter on the subject, written about 1777 ; see *Memoirs of the Med. Soc. Lond.*, vol. i., p. 204.)

(D)   OTHER CONTRIBUTIONS AND MANUSCRIPT WORKS.

Letters and Controversial Papers in the *Critical Review.*

Lectures on Anatomy, Physiology, Surgery, Midwifery, the Art of Embalming, etc., in the manuscript notes of students, preserved in various libraries.

BIOGRAPHY.

Within a few months of Dr. Hunter's death in 1783, an Account of his life was ably and judiciously drawn up by Dr. Samuel Foart Simmons,[1] from full information supplied by Matthew Baillie, John Hunter and other friends. It was read before the Medical Society of Physicians, of which Hunter was, at the time of his death, President, and forms a small book of some seventy pages. All later notices of William Hunter have been based chiefly upon this work.[2] His niece Agnes Baillie left a short record of the family *Pedigree* and traditions concerning her famous uncles, which is preserved among the Hunter-Baillie manuscripts, together with *Reminiscences* of William Hunter, compiled by Dr. Matthew Baillie's only daughter, Mrs. Milligan.

There are good articles under Hunter's name in many of the Encyclopædias, in the *National Dictionary of Biography*, Dr. Munk's *Roll of the Royal College of Physicians*, Dr. Pettigrew's *Medical Portrait Gallery*, and the *Lives of British Physicians* (by Dr. Macmichael); see also *The Gold-headed Cane* by the same author, and Bettany's *Eminent Doctors*. Sir Benjamin C. Brodie delivered the *Hunterian Oration* on William Hunter in 1837, and Dr. Matthews Duncan's *Harveian Address* in 1876 (see *Edinburgh Medical Journal*, June, 1876), gives a most appreciative account of his medical character. Dr. Duncan's *Researches in Obstetrics*, 1868, are also full of allusion to W. Hunter. Accounts of his life and work are likewise to be found in some of the medical periodicals in the course

---

[1] Dr. Simmons (1750—1813) was physician to St. Luke's Hospital and F.R.S. He edited for many years the *London Medical Journal*, etc.

[2] The account of his life in Dr. Andrew Duncan's *Medical Commentaries*, Vol. viii., p. 426, published in Edinburgh, 1783, seems to have been founded on Simmons.

of the nineteenth century. Thus Dr. Robert Lee chose this theme for a discourse to the students of St. George's Hospital in 1844.[1] An excellent pictorial series of articles, with a critical estimate of Hunter's position as a leader in British Medicine, was contributed to the *Medical Times and Gazette* in 1859,[2] and a like series by J. Burgess appeared in the *Medical Circular* next year.[3] Sketches of his life, each illustrated with a portrait, were contained in the *Asclepiad* in 1888, and in the *Practitioner* in 1899. The late Dr. Mather's life of W. Hunter, in *Two Great Scotsmen*, is almost entirely a compilation from Duncan and Simmons, accompanied with two good portraits. Dr. John H. Teacher has prefaced his *Catalogue of the Anatomical and Pathological Preparations* in William Hunter's Museum, published in 1900, by an elegant portrait and *Introduction*, containing a sympathetic account of Hunter's life, with a critical examination of his opinions and discoveries. A lecture by the same author, contributed to the *Glasgow Medical Journal* (July, 1899), includes some further material.

A valuable series of William Hunter's letters is printed in Thomson's *Life of Cullen*, and both in that work and in Glaister's *Dr. William Smellie and his Contemporaries*, there is much information concerning Hunter. Several of Baillie's works contain important allusions to his uncle; and the memoirs of John Hunter by Everard Home, by Foot, by Adams, by Ottley, and especially the most recent, by Stephen Paget (*Masters of Medicine* Series), should be consulted. Other authorities have been cited in the text.[4]

The author would here express his acknowledgments to those who have kindly rendered him assistance in preparing this work. And firstly to the Council of the Royal College of Surgeons, for permission to use the Hunter-Baillie manuscripts, and the author would gladly have coupled with this the name of Mr. J. B. Bailey, B.A., the late Librarian, whose interest in the Hunters was well known. Miss Hunter-Baillie's kindness in giving free access to documents remaining in her own hands deserves warm recognition: well were it if all the family records of the great found

---

[1] *London Medical Gazette*, new series, vol. i., p. 1.

[2] Vol. xviii., pp. 391, 453, 502.

[3] Vol. xvi , pp. 176, etc.

[4] I have not seen the article, *Guglielmo Hunter e la sua scuola* in the *Gazz. Med. Ital. Lomb.*, Milano, 1849.

such worthy and public-spirited custodians. To the learned Curator of the Hunterian Museum, Glasgow, Professor John Young, M.D., are due hearty thanks, as well as to the Under Keepers, Mr. John Young, LL.D. and Dr. John H. Teacher, for many references. Amongst others who have kindly afforded advice or information should be mentioned Mrs. W. Hunter, late of Rothesay, the late Sir James Paget and the late Dr. William Munk.

William Hunter.

William Hunter's portraits are numerous. The principal are by Reynolds, Chamberlen, and Pine. Those by Pine, which are unfortunately the most widely known, are unlike the rest, and exhibit a face of regular features, almost free from lines, and showing little of special character or intelligence. They may belong to an earlier period of life than the others, but the present writer, who has examined nearly all the known examples of William Hunter's portraits in Great Britain, thinks that Pine must have failed to present Hunter's usual aspect. This, as shown by the other portraits and especially by the print preferred by his biographer Simmons, displays a countenance of delicate features, lit up with intelligence and slightly smiling ; —the nose aquiline, with deep naso-labial furrows, and a prominent pointed chin. Native shrewdness, a love of precision, and a polished and engaging address, are suggested by the physiognomy. A cast of his head, taken after death, and now in the Museum, exhibits the same strongly marked features, together with a forehead sloping back to a rounded head of full average size. It may be added that Hunter was a man of slender build, and rather below the middle stature, but there is no reason to think that he was so little as his brother John, who was only five feet two inches in height.

The following is a list of the portraits so far as they are known :—

(1.) Sir Joshua Reynolds painted William, as he painted John Hunter, and although the result bears little comparison with the masterpiece which adorns the Council Room of the Royal College of Surgeons of England, it is a very fine portrait. Two examples are known, one doubtless the replica of the other, and both are in Glasgow ; displayed in the Hunterian Museum, and in the Hall of the Faculty of Physicians and Surgeons, in that city.[1] Hunter is standing at a table, upon which are specimens of the Retroverted Gravid Uterus.[2] A print taken from Freeman's engraving of this portrait forms the frontispiece of the present work.

(2.) A large portrait by Mason Chamberlen, R.A., hangs in the Diploma Gallery of the Royal Academy, London. The figure is seated and full-faced.[3] Collyer's medallion print, after this portrait or a similar one, was preferred by Dr. Simmons (1783), as the best of Hunter's portraits; "it exhibits," he says, " an accurate and striking resemblance of his features." A reproduction will be found at page 63. Hunter is holding up a small model of a skeleton to demonstrate the muscles.

(3.) The best known of Hunter's portraits hangs in the entry-hall of the Royal College of Surgeons of England. It is the work of Pine, and represents the doctor seated at a table, as if in thought, leaning his head on his left hand, the elbow resting on a large book spread open. He wears an ample wig, and the aspect is somewhat feminine. This forms one of a series of portraits of the Hunter family which was presented to the College, with the Hunter-Baillie Manuscripts, by the executors of the late W. Hunter-Baillie in 1895.[4]

(4.) Another portrait by Pine is in the Hunterian Museum, Glasgow. It differs slightly in posture from the last ; Hunter holds a paper before him at the table, and looks away in thought, the face is less feminine, and the coat is highly embroidered.[5]

(5.) By J. Zoffani, R.A., in the Library of the Royal College of Physicians, London, presented by Mr. Bransby

---

[1] The latter portrait is the property of Mrs. William Hunter, late of Rothesay (see footnote, page 3), and is lent by her to the Faculty.

[2] See page 35, and Professor Young's *Catalogue of Pictures, Sculptures, and other works of Art in the University of Glasgow*. The portrait has been reproduced by Annan for Dr. Mather's *Two Great Scotsmen*.

[3] The central part of this portrait was well engraved by Haughton in Cadell's series. There is also a French print.

[4] The portrait was engraved by Thomson for Pettigrew's *Medical Portrait Gallery*, and a print executed by Annan for Dr. Mather's work; other prints are in the *Asclepiad*, 1888, and the *Practitioner*, 1899.

[5] A good print by Annan of this portrait forms the frontispiece to Dr. Teacher's *Catalogue* (see p. 40.)

B. Cooper. Hunter stands lecturing from a paper held up before him, the head turned to face the spectator.

(6.) By the same, in the Council Room of the Royal College of Surgeons. Hunter is demonstrating at a table, upon which are preparations and an inkstand.

(7.) A picture, also by Zoffani, but unfinished in part, hangs on the staircase of the College of Physicians. It formerly belonged to Dr. Matthew Baillie. Hunter is shown lecturing before the Royal Academy.[1]

(8.) Miss Hunter-Baillie possesses a portrait, the artist unknown, but evidently drawn when Hunter was old. It is a full-face figure with white frill and wide collar to the coat.

In the same safe keeping are three fine miniatures. Two are identical, and show the doctor apparently in court dress, a blue coat with gold stripes. The third is an exquisite portrait of Hunter in his old age, attired in a pale grey coat, and holding a skull in his hand. The face is drawn with delicacy and softness. Another fine miniature, known to be the work of Cosway, is in the possession of Dr. Henry Gervis. There is also a medallion in the Hunterian Museum, Glasgow, which is reproduced opposite page 1. A portrait medal has been struck in Hunter's honour, and is figured by Dr. Mather.[2]

---

[1] See page 9, and footnote. There is, I believe, a photograph of this picture at the South Kensington Museum.

[2] There are also a good many prints existing. One of the best was engraved by Thornthwaite in 1780; it represents Hunter lecturing, his elbows on the table, and a pair of spectacles in one hand; a *femur* lies beside him. There are too, a small vignette by W. Read; medallion prints, by Dawe, 1780; Hedges, 1781; and Parry, 1784; others issued by the *European Magazine*, "from a model in the possession of Mr. Pingo of the Tower;" the *Universal Magazine* (Camberledge), both in 1783; besides a portrait published in the same year by J. Walker, and one in 1786 by Dieterich at Göttingen. A large medallion portrait adorned the certificates granted at the Great Windmill Street School of Anatomy. There is also a very singular black and white silhouette (8vo.) of Hunter writing by lamplight in his study, a little man with a big head; a few specimens and books are around him, else the room is bare (see page 48). Most of these engraved portraits are to be seen in the large collections belonging to the Royal College of Surgeons, and the Royal Medical and Chirurgical Society in London, as well as in the Van Kaathoven collection of medical portraits, now in the Surgeon General's Library at Washington, U.S.A.

LONG CALDERWOOD.

BIRTHPLACE OF THE HUNTERS.

The cottage farmhouse purchased by John Hunter, senior, at the beginning of the eighteenth century, and then styled "Calderfield," is yet standing and little changed. It is in the parish of East Kilbride, Lanarkshire, and about seven miles south-east of Glasgow. Here dwelt the said John Hunter and his wife Agnes Paul, and here were born their large family, of whom so many died young of consumption, but out of whom survived William Hunter, Dorothea Baillie, and John Hunter. [See page 2]. The farm is chiefly pasture, and was cut short in its borders by the first John Hunter, who had to sell field after field to supply the needs of his many children. William Hunter, though he visited the old home but once after he went south, restored the bounds of the family estate, buying up the fields around as they came into the market. He left the farm to Matthew Baillie, who honourably gave it up to John Hunter, and after the death without issue of the latter's son, Captain John Banks Hunter, and of his sister, Lady (Agnes) Campbell, it came into the possession of the son of Dr. Baillie, William Hunter-Baillie, as next of kin. The present proprietress, Miss Hunter-Baillie, daughter of the last named, has kindly given the writer some impressions of a visit to her property.

The farm-house is a simple building of two stories, surrounded by trees; the front garden is entered between low pointed stone piers, and a short straight path leads to the small porch before the door. The upstairs room on the left, over the kitchen, is pointed out as that in which the Hunters were born. A large arched bed-recess nearly occupies one side of the room, and still contains an old wooden bedstead; by its side is a cupboard with a window. Dr. Mather's memoir touches on the local features,—the upland pastures and the quiet Scottish scenery, amidst which two great men received the training of their boyhood.[1]

---

[1] The accompanying view of Long Calderwood is taken from a photograph kindly lent by Dr. J. H. Teacher.

LONG CALDERWOOD, *Lanarkshire.*

Birthplace of William and John Hunter.

DR. JOHN FOTHERGILL.[1]

Two letters from Dr. Fothergill to Dr. Hunter are preserved in the Hunter-Baillie Manuscripts. The first is as follows :

" D͟r Doctor,

"I am greatly obliged by thy kind discreet and effectual[ly] application to Lord H. I am not less so to that worthy nobleman, for the part he takes in this affair. It may perhaps never be in my power to make proper acknowledgements to either of you, for even the inclination of serving me.

"I have directed the proper inquirys to be made, respecting Dr. Saunders's connections, and will send them, the moment they come to hand.

"Be kind enough to favour me with a list of the Governors; and if there are any amongst them to whom I can apply, I will do it with pleasure ; it is my duty and I am sure it is my wish to deserve Dr. Hunter's friendship.

"It may perhaps be proper to acquaint Dr. de mainbray, that the corrals are just as they came out of the sea. They may easily be cleaned, by putting them in warm water just acidulated with spirit of sea salt, and then again washing them in fresh warm water. When dry they may be fixed on small suitable pedestals ; and either put up in a glass case to secure them from dust ; or placed upon and down the musæum coverd with glass bells. Some are reserved for Dr. Hunter's musæum, when it is ready to receive them. At present they may lye where they are, as safely, as amidst a thousand Hobgoblins, nightly searching for their scatter'd remains.

---

¹ See page 25.

"Pray D͟r Doctor would it be practicable for Lord H. to
dismiss me with any decency from the stage. I am brought
there to say nothing but what is proper, but to say it and
appear in a ridiculous manner. Is not this as great an
insult upon me, and even upon any character that is
opposite to vice and folly, as can be offerd! Buffoonery
should only be let loose to prey on these; not to render
their opposites in any degree contemptible. If thro'
weakness or indiscretion I slide into mistakes, I bear most
patiently the just chastisement, whether publick or private.
But in this instance I am doubly hurt. I am held up to
the whole town to laugh at, and the people with whom I am
connected likewise. Nor does the faculty in general derive
much benefit from the contempt thrown on an individual,
tho' individuals of the faculty may rejoice at it.

"I am Dr. Hunter's, obliged, respectfull

"J. FOTHERGILL.

"11th Inst."

The date is without month or year. Dr. Fothergill died
in December, 1780. Hunter's connection with the court
began in 1762. "Lord H.," who was evidently Lord
Chamberlain, can only be the Earl of Hertford, who filled
that office from 1766 to 1782. Hunter, as the Queen's physician, probably met him often; and a portrait of Lady
Hertford, who died a year before Hunter, is in the latter's
Museum, together with a letter from Queen Charlotte asking
for a copy of it.

The purpose of Fothergill's application to the Lord
Chamberlain is not stated. It was most likely of a
benevolent nature. Fothergill was no man of courts, and
sought little for himself. When he approached the sovereign
or those in authority it was to plead the cause of peace, of
true religion, or of the sufferings of the oppressed. Thus in
the course of the year 1769 he was engaged with other
Friends in drawing up a letter of advice to members in
America, in addressing Governor Eden on his departure for
Maryland, and in using his influence to defend three
Yorkshire Friends who were excommunicated by the
Archdeacon's Court at Beverley for non-payment of "Clerk's
wages" of eight pence per year to their parish clerk.[1]

---

[1] MS. *Minutes of the Meeting for Sufferings*, Society of Friends, London, 1769.

. The Dr. Saunders mentioned is almost certainly the well-known Dr. William Saunders, F.R.S. (1743-1817), who wrote on Mineral Waters and on various means of treatment.   He was a Scotsman and a friend of Cullen, and settled in London about 1765, when he would be very likely to bring a recommendation to William Hunter.   He was elected Physician to Guy's Hospital 6th May, 1770.   If this letter refers to his application for that post it would probably be written in 1768 or 1769.

Dr. Demainbray (1710-1782), to whom Fothergill had been sending corals, was an Electrician and Astronomer of repute : he discovered the influence of electricity in stimulating the growth of plants.   He was tutor to the Prince of Wales until he came to the throne in 1760, and after that date to the young Queen, so that Hunter would naturally meet him.   In 1768 he was made Astronomer at Kew : it is more likely he would be forming a "Museum" after he had settled at Kew than before, so that the date 1769 would fit well.

Dr Hunter's own Museum is spoken of as not yet ready to receive specimens.   In 1769 he was building his house in Great Windmill Street, and fitting up one magnificent room to contain his collections.

The introduction of the Society of Friends, and of Dr. Fothergill's person in particular, into a play upon the stage seems, from the last paragraph in the letter, to have justly moved the doctor's indignation, which he expresses in his habitual modest and restrained manner of speech.   The severe dress, sedate manner, and strict 'tutoyer' of the Quaker, popular physician as he was, must have been a frequent butt for humour in his day.   Did Hunter succeed, for we may be sure he tried, in inducing the Lord Chamberlain to put an end to this stage ribaldry ? [1]

The second letter is short, and runs thus :

"Lea Hall. 23rd inst.

" Dear Doctor,

"I am yet alive, tho' not quite well. I found myself much reduced, when I got to this place, but have been very quiet, and begin to recover some little strength and spirits. Be kind enough to deliver the inclosed, & introduce me as favourably as possible. It is enough to have

---

[1] Dibdin's play, *The Quaker*, was brought out about 1778.   There may have been a precursor, containing some allusion to Dr. Fothergill, which is not apparent in *The Quaker*, though it might easily be supplied in the acting.

one Anatomist inspecting one's pericranium, but to be under the hands of two such, especially, if the *aestus* [?] of dissecting bites, is terrible to think of. We have had cool, and not unseasonable weather. I have been followed by many letters, and have wrote much. But I have been free from much company. This evening half my holidays is past. But I will forget this, and think only of returning to my Friends in health, & a disposition to rejoice in their happiness.

"Farewel my Friend, & believe me to be very cordially thy admirer.   "J. FOTHERGILL."

The letter is dated from Lea Hall, about four miles from Crewe, in Cheshire, a country house to which Fothergill regularly retired to spend the autumn months in the last sixteen years of his life. His health failed from the continuous pressure of work in London during his later years. This letter may well have been written in 1772, as its expressions accord with a letter of that year quoted by Lettsom in his *Account* of Fothergill.

The enclosure to be delivered by Hunter to some one, and favourably introduced, would seem to have been in response to a request which came through the latter. Perhaps it was John Hunter or Cruikshank who desired the measurements of Fothergill's head for some investigation akin to what was afterwards known as phrenology.[1] The picture is a pleasing one of the old physician, in his country retreat, followed even there by many letters, and though his strength is nearly spent, placid in spirit and playful in humour, thinking ever of others and of their happiness.

Fothergill's medical writings deal with clinical topics. His classical treatise on Putrid Sore-throat passed through five editions between 1748 and 1769.[2] Another paper "of the management proper at the cessation of the Menses" was highly thought of, and has been translated into French; it was republished by the Sydenham Society in 1849.[3]

---

[1] Gall, the founder of phrenology, was born in 1758.

[2] A copy of the first two editions bound together, with marginal pencil notes in Fothergill's handwriting, and an autograph letter from Dr. Cantwell, has been handed down through Fothergill's niece Alice Chorley, Thomas Thompson, Thomas Hancock, M.D., Thomas Bevan, M.D., and T. B. Peacock, M.D., by the last of whom it was presented to the Royal Medical and Chirurgical Society in London.

[3] As Fothergill's dispute with Dr. Leeds, who claimed £500 from him, is alluded to in the *National Dictionary of Biography*, and in *The Georgian Era* (vol. ii., p. 327), where he is severely blamed, it may be mentioned here that an examination of Dr. Leeds' *Appeal* (1773) is sufficient, without hearing Fothergill's side, to convince the reader of the justice of the latter's position.

The Fothergill family can be traced back for three or four centuries in the secluded vales of Westmoreland. John Fothergill's branch moved thence into Wensleydale about 1600. From Sedbergh came Dr. Anthony Fothergill, who died in 1813, aged 78 years : an able physician, and much befriended by his elder namesake, whom indeed, on his death in 1780, he tried to follow in practice in London ; but failing there he went to Bath, where he acquired large business. Anthony Fothergill was an active Fellow of the Medical Society of London, and made many contributions to its transactions : he gave the sum of £500 to its funds.

John Milner Fothergill, M.D. (1841-1888), came also from Westmoreland. He won the Fothergillian medal in 1878 by his essay on the "Antagonistic Action of Therapeutic Agents."

John Fothergill's name is preserved in connection with the Medical Society of London, to which, however, he never belonged, his support having been given to the older "Medical Society of Physicians."[1] Lettsom founded and endowed in 1784 a gold medal in commemoration of Dr. John Fothergill, to be given annually by the Medical Society of London. This Fothergillian medal is now awarded triennially to the author of the best work on some branch of Practical Medicine or Practical Surgery. "*Fothergillius, Medicus, Amicus, Homo*" was to have been the legend around the bust of Fothergill upon the obverse of the medal, but it was altered to, "*Medicus Egregius, Amicis Carus, Omnium Amicus.*"[2]

Fothergill was, I believe, never painted from the life, but there are portraits in the possession of the London College of Physicians (by Hogarth), and of the Medical Society. A very beautiful Wedgwood bust in black ware is also in existence, as well as Cameo portraits and numerous engravings.

---

[1] See Mr. Edmund Owen's *Oration, Trans. Med. Soc. Lond.*, xx., 309. See also *Antea*, p. 21.

[2] The following lines on Fothergill were not improbably composed by Lettsom : —
Cui suas artes, sua dona laetus
Et herbam et Venae salientis ictum
Scire concessit, celerem ct medendi
Delius usum.
See Fothergill's *Works*, by Lettsom, 1783, back of title page; also inscribed under Bartolozzi's portrait of F. in Nichols' *Literary Anecdotes.*

ADDENDA.

DOROTHEA BAILLIE.
(See page 3.)

Dorothea Baillie, sister to W. and J. Hunter, lived to the age of 86 years: her two daughters, Agnes to 99 years and 7 months, and Joanna to 88 years and 5 months respectively. See a memorial tablet in Hampstead Parish Church.

MEMBERSHIP OF THE CORPORATION OF SURGEONS.
(See page 7).

W. Hunter's membership of the Corporation of Surgeons was annulled at his request in 1756, but it does not appear that he paid the appointed fee of 40 guineas for the disfranchisement, as in 1758 he paid a fine of £20, the penalty incurred for joining the College of Physicians without the consent of the Court of Assistants.[1]

FUNERAL OF W. HUNTER.
(See page 15).

"On Saturday, at eight o'clock in the evening, his remains were interred in the vault under St. James' Church [Piccadilly], attended by his nephew (Mr. Baillie) as chief mourner, Dr. Pitcairne, Sir Geo. Baker, Dr. Fordyce, Dr. Heberden, Mr. Cruikshank, Mr. Coombe, Mr. Birmice (his draughtsman), and a few other friends."[2]

"Cold is that hand, which Nature's paths display'd ;
Dead are those lips on which instruction hung ;
Fix'd are those eyes, enlivening all he said ;
For ever mute is that persuasive tongue !"[3]

---

[1] South, *Memorials of the Craft of Surgery in England*, p. 283.
[2] *Gentleman's Magazine*, 1783, p. 366.
[3] Lines on W. Hunter, quoted by Wadd, *Nugae Chirurgicae*, 1824, p. 230.

INDEX

2 ???? ??????
???????? ??

???? ?????
???? 2012

Lightning Source UK Ltd.
Milton Keynes UK
UKHW02f2006200818
327529UK00009B/305/P